GOD'S MAKEOVER PLAN

GOD'S MAKEOVER PLAN

Transforming Our Attitudes about Inner and Outer Beauty

NANCY EICHMAN

GOSPEL ADVOCATE COMPANY
NASHVILLE, TENNESSEE

Published by Gospel Advocate Co.
1006 Elm Hill Pike, Nashville, TN 37210
http://www.gospeladvocate.com

ISBN 0-89225-380-0

To my husband Phil –
you're the best.

*W*arm thanks to some lovely people:

Connie Pyles, Jane McWhorter and Phil Eichman for their assistance in critiquing the manuscript.

Belva Bellcock, Ernestine Brown, Roberta Brown, Bonnie Bryan, Debbie Chaffin, Paula Eichman, Mildred Ferrell, Sherrie Ferrell, Randa Ford, Glenna Harrison, Kathy Henton, Gail Hutchison, LaVera McCord, Jen McWhorter, Gail Miller, Joy Miller, Marie Roberson, Judy Tebbs, Dianna Teel, Ellen Welker and Carolyn Walker for taking the time to obtain results for the Beauty Attitude Survey.

Mibra Chaffin and the memory of Cecil Chaffin, my parents, for cheering me on.

Phil Eichman, my husband, and John and Amy Eichman, my children, for their love and encouragement.

Contents

*A*N INSIDE-OUT JOB

> *"Therefore I urge you, brothers, in view of God's mercy, to offer your bodies as living sacrifices, holy and pleasing to God – this is your spiritual act of worship. Do not conform any longer to the pattern of this world, but be transformed by the renewing of your mind. Then you will be able to test and approve what God's will is – his good, pleasing and perfect will."*
>
> Romans 12:1–2

*O*NE OF MY FAVORITE features in women's magazines and TV shows is "The Makeover." It amazes me how transformed a woman can look in a short time when experts move in with all their equipment and know-how. By coordinating the right makeup, hairstyle and clothing, the makeover looks great! Usually she has a frowning, frumpy "before" photograph and a radiant, attractive "after."

But something else happens. The participant tells how her outside change makes her feel different inside – more adventurous and confident to face new challenges. The outside altered state begins to transform the inside. The new look produces a new outlook.

We as Christian women go through a spiritual makeover. Our changing process, however, begins on the inside and moves outward. As we submit our hearts to God, He begins a deliberate but gradual transformation. This evolving process takes a lifetime – no quick-fix here! It would be nice if we would rise from the waters of baptism as mature women of our utmost potential. Instead, we come up new creatures, clean and innocent like babies who have a lot of growing to do (2 Corinthians 5:17; 1 Peter 2:2).

So God's beauty makeover is an inside-out job. The inner beauty that the Lord bestows will manifest itself in an outer glow and happiness that no one can mistake. Peace within translates to a peaceful, calm expression without. A joyful spirit brings forth a smile. Love in the heart speaks in a kind, considerate voice. No, salvation does not change the shape of our nose or our ears, but it does change the shape of our spiritual heart.

In both spiritual and physical makeovers, attitudes are involved. Our attitudes must undergo a transformation before we can change. That is what this book is about – a makeover in our attitudes about inner and outer beauty. I initially thought the topic of beauty might be a frivolous Bible study subject. Then I began to hear of Christian teens starving themselves in a tragic effort to meet false standards of beauty. Other believers fight a battle with obesity that seems out of control. Often conversations even among women in the church focus on daily struggles with dieting, aging, competition or low body image. These issues at times prevent us from being effective in our walk with God. True, these are physical problems, but at their root often lie attitude problems. I began to search the Scriptures for answers, and I was not disappointed!

Granted, the Bible doesn't talk about body image, anorexia or dieting per se, although it does specifically address clothes, exercise and gluttony. But the more I delved into the principles involved in these topics, the more convinced I became that God *does* provide "everything we need for life and godliness" (2 Peter 1:3). The Bible is our all-sufficient source of wisdom.

At the end of each chapter is a set of "Inside Out" questions that pertain to topics discussed in the chapter. After the questions, there is a section titled "The Way It Was" that provides a glimpse of some aspect of beauty in Bible times. After Chapter 13, this section changes to "The Way It Is," an informal survey of beauty attitudes among 100 women in the church. This section offers insight into current views on beauty topics from a Christian perspective.

As you begin, know that God offers to transform your attitudes about beauty. Let Him assure you of your worth, independent of the world's values. Let Him make you over – inside and out!

Chapter 1

*W*HAT A DIFFERENCE!

*"I will give you a
new heart and
put a new spirit
in you; I will
remove from you
your heart of
stone and give
you a heart of
flesh."*

(Ezekiel 36:26)

*O*UR SOCIETY IS BUILT on change. Many
of us move every few years. We transfer jobs.
We marvel at scientific breakthroughs that
make new technology possible. Telecom-
munication, for example, is expanding so quickly we can barely keep up. Nothing stands still.
We anticipate new and improved products. We
rush to be the first on the block to own the
latest gadget. We trade in perfectly good cars
for the latest model. Fashion dictates that our
styles change every season. We long for a new
look. We tire of the same old thing. No wonder beauty makeovers are popular.

God and Change

In this world of breakneck speed and change,
God is an anchor, a rock who does not change
(Malachi 3:6; James 1:17). It is heartening to
know that we can lean on God and His Son
Jesus, who are "the same yesterday and today
and forever" (Hebrews 13:8).

Quite the opposite is true of mankind. The
desire for change seems almost instinctive for
us. Ever since Adam and Eve could not wait to
try a new fruit, humans have been trying to

change God's laws to fit their own criteria. The Israelites had an insatiable appetite for something different. They wanted to change addresses (leaving for the Promised Land, then wanting to return to Egypt), change food (demanding manna and quail, then getting sick of it) and change leaders (grumbling against Moses to the point he thought they would stone him). After many generations, they wanted a new kind of leader – a king. Sadly, many also changed their allegiance from the true God to the gods of the nations around them.

God saw that people needed change all right – a change of heart and spirit. So the God who does not change sent His Son to offer the ultimate change. Starting with the Jews and eventually including the Gentiles, Jesus offered a radically different lifestyle. His teachings were so different that the Pharisees and Sadducees, the religious leaders of the day, thought Him a rebel. But to people who accepted and obeyed His teaching, Jesus gave a revolutionary way of life. He told them, for example, that for a person to be truly great, he must change and become like a little child (Matthew 18:3-4). In the Sermon on the Mount (5:21-48), Jesus told them:

It was said ...	But I tell you ...
Don't murder.	Don't be angry, but settle your differences.
Don't commit adultery.	Don't look at a woman with lust in your heart.
An eye for an eye and a tooth for a tooth.	Don't take revenge, but go the second mile.
Love your neighbor and hate your enemies.	Love your enemies.

These principles were so different that in the next few years the world was turned upside down by Jesus' apostles, spreading the "full message of this new life" (Acts 5:20).

God Can Change Us

The most amazing thing is that God can change us – and He can start doing it now! If we are willing, He can transform us from our present state into something He can use, something much better and more beautiful. In baptism, we become new creatures (Romans

6:3-8; 2 Corinthians 5:17). Sometimes, however, we may underestimate the great power of God to change us. If we have grown up in a religious home with godly parents, we might forget how lost we would be without His saving grace. Often we don't know how far we've come with God because we don't remember how lost we were without Him.

Just like the "before" and "after" of a beauty makeover, stark contrasts between our lost and saved spiritual conditions can be seen. Isaiah painted a graphic picture of the change God can bring about in our lives: "Though your sins are like scarlet, they shall be as white as snow; though they are red as crimson, they shall be like wool" (Isaiah 1:18).

Spiritual transformation is a common theme in the New Testament. Consider these examples:

Before	*After*
Lost	Found (Luke 15:32)
Old	New (2 Corinthians 5:17)
Enslaved	Free (Galatians 5:13)
In the world	In Christ (Ephesians 1:3, 7)
Hopeless	Hopeful (Ephesians 2:12)
Far away	Near (Ephesians 2:13)
Dead	Alive (Colossians 2:13)
Empty	Abundant (1 Peter 1:18)
In darkness	In the light (1 Peter 2:9)

Paul further described this metamorphosis that takes place in Ephesians 4:22-24:

You were taught, with regard to your former way of life, to put off your old self, which is being corrupted by its deceitful desires; to be made new in the attitude of your minds; and to put on the new self, created to be like God in true righteousness and holiness.

In other words, Paul is saying, get rid of the old life and start again with a fresh way of looking at things – God's way! Taking on God's way of looking at things is the beginning of God's makeover plan for us.

God, Our Makeover Master

The woman wanting a spiritual beauty makeover might wonder, "Am I good enough? What can be done with me? How can I be made beautiful?" But the true makeover expert can take any woman, with her strengths and weaknesses, and make her lovelier. We have the opportunity to be made over by God. God takes us as we are and makes us spiritually beautiful.

The hand of an expert is needed to enhance the true outer beauty in a person. The expert has to be trusted to do what is best for the one being made over. Likewise, it takes the Master's hand to make a true change in our hearts. This transformation begins when we allow Him to take full control of our lives.

In her book *Beauty and the Best*, Debra Evans writes,

Transformed. Renewed. Born again. Forgiven. Accepted. Baptized unto Christ's death that we might live with Him in eternity. We've heard of these things many times before, but what do they have to do with beauty? *Everything.* If we continually worry about the way we look or what we're wearing, focus too much on our weight and whether or not to go on a diet, berate our appearance while criticizing the appearances of others, compare ourselves to one another as we compete against our closest friends, get hung up on working out after feeling guilty for pigging out, and take pride in our "successes" after becoming depressed over any "failures" in this area, haven't we somehow forgotten something? You bet we have. Until we are broken of our dependence on our own self-images, we cannot fully embrace the image of God in ourselves or each other. [1]

Just as a cosmetic makeover can make a dramatic difference, so God can make phenomenal changes in our lives. Both our inner and outer selves can be changed. In the remaining chapters, we will examine how "renewing our minds" with different attitudes can affect the whole spectrum of beauty in our lives.

Inside Out

1. In his epistles, Paul offers several contrasts to show God's working in the Christian. Fill in the afters.

Before   *After*

1 Corinthians 6:9-11

Wicked   _____

Sexually immoral   _____

Idolaters   _____

Adulterers   _____

Male prostitutes   _____

Homosexual offenders   _____

Thieves   _____

Greedy   _____

Drunkards   _____

Slanderers   _____

Swindlers   _____

Ephesians 2:1-6, 10-13, 19

Dead in transgressions   _____

Followed the ways of this world   _____

Disobedient   _____

Gratifying cravings of sinful nature _____

Objects of wrath   _____

Separate from Christ   _____

Excluded from citizenship in Israel _____

Foreigners to the covenants of the promise

Without hope   _____

Without God in the world   _____

Far away   _____

Foreigners and aliens   _____

Colossians 1:21-22

Alienated from God   _____

Enemies in your minds   _____

Evil behavior   _____

2. Peter also contrasted God's transformation in His people. Fill in the "afters."

Before   *After*

1 Peter 2:10

Not a people   _____

Not received mercy   _____

The Way It Was

ℬALDHEADED AND BEARDED LADIES

*O*vid, the Roman poet, wrote, "There is nothing graceful about becoming bald."[2] Baldness might come to a woman from carrying heavy articles on her head as in Ezekiel 29:18: "Every head was rubbed bare." The condition might also come from disease, as in Isaiah 3:17: "Therefore the Lord will bring sores on the heads of the women of Zion; the Lord will make their scalps bald."

A woman could dedicate her hair by shaving it off in a Nazirite vow. Her hair was allowed to grow until the end of the vow, when it was shaved and offered as a sacrifice (Numbers 6:1-21). Hair could also be shaved off on occasions of deep sorrow, death or desolation as in the destruction of Jerusalem. "Shave your heads in mourning for the children in whom you delight; make yourselves as bald as the vulture, for they will go from you into exile" (Micah 1:16).[3]

When an Israelite man was attracted to a beautiful foreign woman and wanted to bring her to his home as a wife, she had to shave her head, trim her nails, and put aside the clothes she was wearing when she was captured. After a month of mourning for her parents, she could become the wife of the Israelite (Deuteronomy 21:12-13). At their wedding, her hair would be about an inch long.

Because the Egyptians valued cleanliness and coolness, they kept their hair short or shaved and wore elaborate wigs in public. One Egyptian queen, Hatshepsut, opted as well for a ceremonial beard held on by straps![4]

Chapter 2

REFLECTING WHOSE IMAGE?

"We see the most proper image of the beauty of Christ when we see beauty in the human soul."

Jonathan Edwards[1]

HAVE YOU EVER SEEN yourself in a funhouse mirror, the kind that waves and dips? At one place on the mirror, you look huge. Move a bit and your reflection is very thin. Your actual size remains the same, but the image in the mirror distorts your appearance depending on where you look, and you can't see who you really are.

The world can be just like that mirror. If we depend on the world to see what is truly beautiful, we see a distorted image. Our ideas of spiritual and physical beauty can become a little confused. Things are not what they seem. Myriad reflections bombard us from all sides, clamoring for our attention and our money. The world's mirror is full of images. How many of them can we trust?

Manufacturers. Manufacturers turn designers' dreams into reality, whether they are the latest style of clothes, hair dryer or nail polish. They tell us what length to wear our skirts, what seasonal color is in, and what look is out. They make us think we must have what is hot, and that can change overnight. Fashion is fickle.

Merchants. Merchants tie a bow on their package, so to speak. They play music to shop by and arrange attractive displays to entice us. They make malls windowless and clockless so we won't know how long we've shopped. They make it simple to spend our money with easy credit, free parking and convenient shopping hours. No wonder it is so easy to spend so much in so little time!

Media. Television, radio, movies, billboards, magazines, newspapers and now cyberspace – the media are everywhere. Anywhere we look we face a beautiful body trying to sell us everything from toothpaste to cars. TV personalities and movie stars give credibility to products because of their celebrity status.

Men. The opinions of our husbands, boyfriends and male associates are very important to us, sometimes too important. A compliment can make our day, while a put-down can devastate us. Our culture coaxes males to believe they can decide what is beautiful in a woman, and that rubs off on us.[2]

Models. Gracing the covers of women's magazines, models are the epitome of what our culture says we should look like, but often can't. Who can always be tall and thin with perfect nails, skin, makeup, hair and color-coordinated clothes? We think we can never measure up to such impossible standards. Even those of us who are tall and thin can't have skin that is air-brushed to perfection.

If such reflections from society's mirror are setting us up for failure, why do we even look at it? Unfortunately, we would have to live deep in a remote jungle in the Amazon rain forest not to be affected by American society. How, then, can we live in the world without being permeated by its values?

A Different Mindset

We live in the world, but we don't have to love all the things in the world (1 John 2:15-17). We can be influenced by the world's mode, but we don't have to be entrapped by its mold. Paul urged the Romans, "Do not conform any longer to the pattern of this world, but be transformed by the renewing of your mind" (Romans 12:2). A renewed mind – a change of thinking – that's the beginning of doing God's will and being acceptable to Him. We must have a different mindset about beauty inside and outside, before we can break away from the false values our culture dictates. This different mindset leads to a changed life. About this makeover, Paul states, "[Y]ou have taken off your old self with its practices and have put on the new self, which is being renewed in knowledge in the image of its Creator" (Colossians 3:9-10). The new self of the Christian becomes more and more like the image of the Creator. Paul again emphasized:

> You were taught, with regard to your former way of life, to put off your old self, which is being corrupted by its deceitful desires; to be made new in the attitude of your minds; and to put on the new self, created to be like God in true righteousness and holiness (Ephesians 4:22-24).

We see here that we were created to be like God, not the world. This new self is being made over with God as our designer and image-molder.

The Bible's Mirror

When we look at the Bible as a mirror to find out what we should look like, it reflects different images than culture – the most prominent being God Himself. Throughout Scripture we see the nature of God and how we can be like Him. We don't see a physical description of God, but we see what He is like by what He does.

God "created man in His own image, in the image of God He created him; male and female He created them" (Genesis 1:27). God breathed into them the breath of life, and they became living souls. Just like a child reflects the physical image of one or both of his parents, so men and women are like God spiritually in that they have eternal souls. God gave this eternal capacity only to people; no other creatures would live forever.

Adam and Eve soon were marred by sin, failing to live up to God's image in them. As time went on, man wandered so far from God in sin that he forgot the spiritual nature of his Maker. People modeled their own gods out of clay, wood, stone and metal to have a visible representation of the deity they worshiped, although they did not know who God really was (Acts 17:23).

The abuses of idolatry in other religions ranged from sexual immorality to the sacrifice of children, but still the Israelites wanted graven images of their own. The true God abhorred graven images, specifically commanding in the Ten Commandments that the Israelites make no gods or graven images (Exodus 20:4-6). God's anger burned time after time against His people when they were drawn away by idolatry.

Why did God's people need an image of Him, anyway? Could they not see Him in other ways? In the wilderness, whether by nightly pillar of fire or daily cloud, He was leading them. With His miraculous might, He brought water out of rock, food out of the desert, and victory over a mighty Egyptian army by providing a path through the Red Sea.

Isaiah also asked why God's people needed an image of Him in Isaiah 40:18-26. In one magnificent show of power, God overcame Baal's prophets on Mount Carmel. After such a victory, God came to Elijah in a whisper, perhaps saying, "You don't need an idol to see Me. Can't you see what I'm like through what I do? Can't you 'see' Me?" He wanted them to look beyond the physical to the spiritual. That's what God is – spirit – and He wants His people to worship Him that way (John 4:24).

But God's people drifted further away, failing to discern Him through His mighty acts. They needed a closer view, a clearer focus. So God sent to Earth in physical form His nearest and dearest – His Son, Jesus. Through Jesus, man could see God up close and personal. Jesus said, "Anyone who has seen me has seen the Father" (John 14:9). John wrote, "The Word became flesh and made his dwelling among us. We have seen his glory, the glory of the One and Only, who came from the Father, full of grace and truth" (1:14).

The Bible doesn't describe Jesus' physical characteristics. The closest look we have of His outward appearance is Isaiah's prophecy of the Messiah in Isaiah 53:2: "He had no beauty or majesty to attract us to him, nothing in his appearance that we should desire him." The throngs didn't flock to Jesus for His handsome features. They found a deeper attraction – a beauty of the soul that filled their deepest longings. Jesus' mercy, love, compassion and wisdom served as a magnet to people from all walks of life.

So now people could see God through Jesus. "The Son is the radiance of God's glory and the exact representation of his being, sustaining all things by his powerful word" (Hebrews 1:3). They could touch Him and hear His voice and see He was alive. In 1 John 1:1-4, John emphasized this to the Gnostic unbelievers – heretics who denied that Divinity could take on flesh.

But some people didn't want to see God because He exposed their ugliness (sin), so they killed Jesus. However, they underestimated God's power, and Jesus rose triumphantly over Satan and the grave. Even after death, people could still "see" God in Jesus as indicated by Thomas who after seeing the resurrected Jesus said, "My Lord and my God" (John 20:28).

Reflecting His Beauty

After His resurrection, Jesus returned to heaven to be with the Father. How then can God be seen through Jesus today? In the Word and in a living reflection in His disciples. To us God gave the power to reflect the beauty of His Son. When we become God's children, we reflect Jesus. The world sees Him through our lives. Of course we aren't perfect, but when someone sees Jesus in us, they have seen what God is like.

When Moses received the Ten Commandments and came close to seeing God Himself, "his face was radiant because he had spoken with the Lord" (Exodus 34:29). Paul wrote about this reflection beautifully in 2 Corinthians 3:13-18:

> We are not like Moses, who would put a veil over his face to keep the Israelites from gazing at it while the radiance was fading away. But their minds were made dull, for to this day the same veil remains when the old covenant is read. It has not been removed, because only in Christ is it taken away. Even to this day when Moses is read, a veil covers their hearts. But when anyone turns to the Lord, the veil is taken away. Now the Lord is the Spirit, and where the Spirit of the Lord is, there is freedom. And we, who with unveiled faces all reflect the Lord's glory, are being transformed into his likeness with ever-increasing glory, which comes from the Lord, who is the Spirit.

Such spiritual radiance can be ours the closer we get to God and the more we reflect the Lord's glory. We were made in God's image. We can also be made *over* in His image. We don't have to succumb to artificial molds of fashion or beauty. We can be the genuine article, reflecting an image that is ever living and real.

Inside Out

1. Give examples of how the images reflected by manufacturers, merchants, media, men and models affect our views of ourselves.

2. Who in the Bible set up graven images for God's people to worship?

3. Who saw Jesus after He was resurrected, and how did they know He was real?

4. What did the Gnostics believe, and why did John try to convince them of Jesus' humanity (1 John 1:1-4)?

5. God allowed Moses to see His back, but what was he not permitted to see (Exodus 33:23)?

6. In what ways did God create male and female in His own image (Genesis 1:26-27; 9:6)?

7. How does Psalm 8:3-8 demonstrate the unique purpose for which God created man?

8. What vivid contrast does Paul make between the idols of Athens and the living God (Acts 17:22-31)?

9. How is Jesus the image of God (Colossians 1:15-20)?

10. How did God contrast His creative power to the foolishness of making graven images in Isaiah 44?

$\mathcal{M}$IRROR, MIRROR

"$\mathcal{N}$ow we see but a poor reflection as in a mirror" (1 Corinthians 13:12). Paul knew the inadequacy of the mirrors of his day. Mirrors made of glass did not appear until late Roman times.[3] Before, they were made of highly polished bronze, copper, gold, silver or electrum (an alloy of gold and silver), each capable of reflecting a person's face.[4]

Ancient mirrors have been excavated with women's apparel and jewelry. They were usually round, often having a handle of ivory or wood. The handles could be ornately decorated with engraved circles, dots and spirals. They were highly prized and exchanged as gifts among royalty.[5]

The laver or wash basin of the tabernacle was made by melting down the metal mirrors of the women who served at its entrance (Exodus 38:8). These mirrors may have been treasured possessions of Hebrew women who asked for gifts as they were leaving Egypt in the Exodus.[6]

Mirrors also are used figuratively in Scripture. James tells of one who looks in a mirror and then forgets what he looks like – just like a person who listens to the Word but does not do what it says (James 1:23). In Job 37:18 Elihu asked, "[C]an you join [God] in spreading out the skies, hard as a mirror of cast bronze?" He probably was referring to the brightness of the sky resembling polished metal.[7]

Chapter 3

DEDICATING OUR TEMPLES

"It is not the worship of beauty we need so much as the beauty of holiness."

Michael Fairless[1]

TODAY, IMPRESSIVE ribbon-cutting dedication ceremonies draw quite an array of dignitaries, reporters, cameras and overall hoopla. But it would be difficult to rival the dedication of Solomon's temple in Jerusalem.

Before thousands of Israel's citizens, King Solomon knelt in prayer to thank God for His help in the past and to request forgiveness for future sins. So many cattle and sheep were sacrificed that they couldn't be counted. Singers and 120 trumpeters, accompanied by cymbals, harps and lyres, joined in unison to praise the Lord. At the end of Solomon's prayer, fire from heaven consumed the offerings and the glory of the Lord filled the temple. All the people fell with their faces to the ground when they saw God's power (2 Chronicles 5-7).

Only the best was good enough for Solomon's temple. David, Solomon's father, asked the Israelites to bring their gold, silver, jewels and other offerings to provide for the Lord's house. Rich and poor gave what they had, and their leaders were pleased and praised God. When God specified the particular trappings for the temple, He didn't leave details

27

to chance. During the seven years it took to build the temple, detailed instructions were followed. Skilled craftsmen were called in to produce the best quality engravings and curtains with the finest materials. God didn't want this elaborate structure to go into disrepair. He appointed the Levites to maintain the facilities as well as perform their priestly duties.

Adorning Our Temple

In the New Testament the idea of the value, care and adornment that went along with the temple led to its being representative of the Christian's body: "Do you not know that your body is a temple of the Holy Spirit, who is in you, whom you have received from God? You are not your own: you were bought at a price. Therefore honor God with your body" (1 Corinthians 6:19-20).

How are we honoring God with our bodies? When we consider the planning and maintenance that went into the temple, we get a sense of what should go into the care and dressing of our bodies. Would God have been happy with a temple of leftover lumber barely standing up? Or would He have been delighted with a ramshackle building that was cheaply and quickly constructed with little forethought? No, the Lord wanted the best that His people could offer. Likewise, we as His people today should take care of our bodies and our appearance. We don't have to wear the most expensive clothes, but that does not give us the excuse to look sloppy or dirty.

Some Christians excuse their unkempt clothing and messy appearance with the excuse that "God makes me beautiful inside, and my outside doesn't matter." They figure that they don't need to spend any time or effort on their outer selves. They think like the backwoods woman who claimed, "If God had wanted me to cut my toenails and wash my hair, He would have given me toenail clippers and shampoo!" The inside is most important, but we don't want to forget the outside!

Some people have seen Paul's instruction to women in 1 Timothy 2:9-10 as a rationale for women to pay no attention to their appearance. In this passage, he exhorts women to "dress modestly, with decency and propriety, not with braided hair or gold or pearls or expensive clothes, but with good deeds, appropriate for women who profess to worship God."

Paul assumes that women should take the time and effort to adorn themselves. The question is "How?" Rather than showing off extravagant braids, gold, pearls or expensive clothes as was prevalent in Paul's day, he urged women to dress with modesty and good sense. This implies that Christian women could dress in the current fashion if it was not indecent or extreme. The Christian woman today does not have to look awkward or old-fashioned, for then she will look conspicuous. By dressing appropriately and in good taste, she can concentrate on giving glory to God instead of wearing fancy or imprudent clothes and drawing attention to herself.[2]

God's Spirit Within

Solomon was wise enough to know that the temple only symbolized God's presence. The Almighty could not be contained in one building, no matter how magnificent. Solomon asked God, "But will God really dwell on earth with men? The heavens, even the highest heavens, cannot contain you. How much less this temple I have built!" (2 Chronicles 6:18). Stephen echoed this sentiment in Acts 7:48: "However, the Most High does not live in houses made by men."

Why was the temple really important? It wasn't the physical presence of the structure that made it special but rather who dwelt inside – the Spirit of God. The mighty God whose name was too holy for the Jews to mention had a dwelling place close to His people. In a similar way, our bodies are not special because of their outside appearance. Although we must take care of the outside, our bodies are important because of what dwells inside – the Spirit of God. Paul exclaims:

> You, however, are controlled not by the sinful nature but by the Spirit, if the Spirit of God lives in you. And if anyone does not have the Spirit of Christ, he does not belong to Christ. But if Christ is in you, your body is dead because of sin, yet your spirit is alive because of righteousness. And if the Spirit of him who raised Jesus from the dead is living in you, he who raised Christ from the dead will also give life to your mortal bodies through his Spirit, who lives in you (Romans 8:9-11).

Yet the very fact that the Spirit lives in us shows how special our bodies really are. It is truly beyond our human understanding that God's Spirit can dwell within our physical bodies.

Destroying God's Temple

Sadly, Solomon's magnificent structure didn't last. The temple was destroyed by King Nebuchadnezzar of Babylon, and the Jews were led into Babylonian captivity. Years later, Cyrus, king of Persia, allowed a remnant of Jews to return and rebuild the temple in Jerusalem. Ultimately, the temple was rebuilt twice and played a crucial role in the lives and religion of the Jewish people.

Centuries later, Paul spoke of people destroying their bodies, the temple of God. Many Corinthians in Paul's day thought that the soul of man was all that mattered and because the body was unimportant it could be abused by food, drink or sex.[3] They wanted to separate the spirit and body. But Paul told them to keep their souls and their bodies from contamination (2 Corinthians 7:1). He asked them, "Don't you know that you yourselves are God's temple and God's Spirit lives in you? If anyone destroys God's temple, God will destroy him; for God's temple is sacred, and you are that temple" (1 Corinthians 3:16-17).

God loves the whole of man – the body and the spirit. In fact, Paul compares the care and nurture of the body and spirit with Christ and the church: "After all, no one ever hated his own body, but he feeds and cares for it, just as Christ does the church – for we are members of his body" (Ephesians 5:29-30). Knowing how much Jesus loves the body, the church for which He died, helps us to understand the respect and value we should confer on our bodies.

Today some people believe their bodies are inherently evil and animalistic. When they view their bodies in this way, they feel free to sin. Others punish their "bad" bodies by severe prohibitions or self-abuse.[4] They believe they must place severe restrictions on their bodies and deny themselves every source of pleasure, even wholesome ones. Some women hate their bodies so much they have been known to cut or burn themselves, reopen wounds, pull their hair, or even break their bones.

Clearly God does not condone hurting a body He so masterfully created. Harsh treatment of our bodies is not the answer to controlling our sinful ways (Colossians 2:23). Sin originates in the heart and mind, not in the body (Mark 7:20-23). If only regulating our bodies would keep us from sin, we would have an easier time keeping pure. Rather than totally denying our bodies, we are called to a more balanced approach of disciplining them (1 Corinthians 6:12).[5]

Glorious Bodies

David wrote, "I praise you because I am fearfully and wonderfully made; your works are wonderful, I know that full well" (Psalm 139:14). This fearfully and wonderfully made body is truly a masterpiece of grand design. The average woman's body contains 206 bones and more than 600 muscles. For every one square inch of female skin there are 12 feet of nerves, 15 feet of blood vessels, 1,500 sensory receptors, 100 oil glands, 650 sweat glands, and more than 3 million cells. We shed and renew our layer of skin about every 28 days. It has been claimed that dead skin accounts for 90 percent of household dust. There are approximately 100,000 hairs on her head, but only God knows the actual count (Luke 12:7).[6]

God demonstrated how special our mortal bodies are by sending His Son to Earth. Jesus came and died in a flesh-and-blood body just like ours. "But now he has reconciled you by Christ's physical body through death to present you holy in his sight, without blemish and free from accusation" (Colossians 1:22).

Ultimately, we dedicate our temples daily by doing the will of Christ. Paul writes, "The body is not meant for sexual immorality, but for the Lord, and the Lord for the body" (1 Corinthians 6:13). Rather than using our bodies for ourselves, our whole purpose for living is to glorify Him in our bodies. "Do not offer the parts of your body to sin, as instruments of wickedness, but rather offer yourselves to God, as those who have been brought from death to life; and offer the parts of your body to him as instruments of righteousness" (Romans 6:13). While some people devalue the physical body, God values it by showing its purpose – to glorify Him.

One day, however, the body will pass away in death and return to dust. So we don't want to think too much of our bodies; they are just a temporary dwelling (2 Corinthians 5:1-10). Our spirits will live forever. We have a more permanent dwelling waiting after the death of the body. "But our citizenship is in heaven. And we eagerly await a Savior from there, the Lord Jesus Christ, who, by the power that enables him to bring everything under his control, will transform our lowly bodies so that they will be like his glorious body" (Philippians 3:20-21).

Our bodies, with all their wonderful complexities, are a grand dwelling place for God. We must treat them with the same honor and respect God's people once showed to the temple. We can even look forward to an even more glorious body prepared for us in heaven. How wonderful that will be.

Inside Out

1. Describe the dedication ceremony of Solomon's temple.

2. What materials were used to build the temple, and where did they come from?

3. Whom did Solomon use to build the temple? Why do you think no hammer, chisel or other iron tool was heard at the temple site while it was being built (1 Kings 5:13-18; 6:7)?

4. When would God make the temple a byword and an object of ridicule among all people (2 Chronicles 7:19-22)?

5. Why was the temple really important? Why are our temples important?

6. Because our insides are most important, does that give us an excuse to forget our outside appearance?

7. What was Paul's emphasis on women's appearance in 1 Timothy 2:9-10?

8. How are some ways people can destroy their temples?

9. What did the Corinthians of Paul's day believe about the soul and the body?

10. What rises to become a holy temple according to Ephesians 2:19-22?

$\mathcal{S}$WEET-SMELLING SAVORS

$\mathcal{W}$hen the woman broke the alabaster jar and poured the expensive perfume on Jesus' head (Mark 14:3-9), she was performing a task that Simon the Leper, Jesus' host, had forgotten. In that day, when deodorants were unknown, a customary courtesy in Palestine's hot, dry climate was to anoint guests' heads with oil to soothe the skin and provide a sweet fragrance. Despite criticism, Jesus commended the woman's financial sacrifice – a year's wages.

Perfumes and ointments were made by apothecaries, perfumers, confectioners, priests or individuals.[7] Kings perfumed their furniture and apparel, and they usually required the services of perfumers (1 Samuel 8:13).

The perfumers did not distill the essence like modern manufacturers. They compressed fresh flowers in a bag, soaked them in fat releasing the essential oils, and constantly changed them. To speed up the process, they commonly dipped them into hot fats at 65° C. Various countries and regions supplied ingredients for perfumes: Palestine – stacte and saffron; the Red Sea – onycha; Somaliland – frankincense; Ceylon – cinnamon; Arabia – bdellium, frankincense and myrrh; Persia – galbanum; India – aloes and nard.[8]

Perfumes were originally used for religious purposes. In the Old Testament, two recipes for sacred perfume and incense were specified not for personal use but exclusively for the tabernacle (Exodus 30:22-38). Oils were used to anoint new kings (2 Kings 9:3), the sick (James 5:14) and the dead (2 Chronicles 16:14; Mark 14:8; Luke 23:56; John 19:39-42).[9]

Perfumes and ointments also became useful for personal hygiene (Esther 2:12; Proverbs 7:17; 27:9; Isaiah 57:9). Their use for this purpose was so customary that their absence signified mourning (Deuteronomy 28:40; Ruth 3:3; 2 Samuel 14:2; Daniel 10:3; Amos 6:6; Micah 6:15).[10]

$\mathcal{B}$ORN A BEAUTY OR BORN-AGAIN BEAUTY?

"On a purely physical level, beauty is our reflection in the mirror. On a deeper level, it is our ability to accept that reflection."

Victoria Jackson[1]

$\mathcal{F}$OR BETTER OR WORSE, we are born with our bodies. Adam and Eve, created in perfection by God's own hand, were pronounced "very good." Sadly, we often don't judge our own bodies so favorably. Our bodies are extraordinary machines, capable of doing so many things. Intricate internal processes occur without our giving them a thought. God showed His great genius in creating humans, a combination of free-thinking soul and flesh. Somehow we often miss the marvel of His creation and sell ourselves short.

Many women think that the features they were born with are not good enough. This is especially true with women in the United States. According to a Kinsey Institute survey, American women "have more negative feelings about their bodies than women in any other culture studied."[2] Another study found that in a group of average-size women, only those 10 pounds underweight were content with their figures.[3] The media and beauty industry promote going to any extreme to change oneself to fit the ideal. Characteristics that make ethnic groups distinct, such as noses

35

and eyes of a certain shape, are reshaped to meet Anglo-Western norms.[4] Cosmetic surgery, now termed "body sculpting," supposedly can correct any "problem" and give anyone a perfect body. One doctor even promised to shorten women's height by sawing off their leg bones![5]

Although each of us is born distinctly unique, many aspire to a perfect body with specified measurements that elude the average woman. Ironically, the dimensions of this perfection change with the times. The fleshy Rubenesque body of the 17th century is a far cry from today's thin-is-in look. One model admits that today's ideal "is a muscular body with big breasts. Nature doesn't make women like that."[6] In the face of all these standards of beauty, we often believe we must either be born beautiful or spend our lives working to look that way. Because our attitudes toward our bodies have a lot to do with how effective our lives will be, this widespread dissatisfaction with our appearance has a negative effect on our realizing the abundant life Jesus promised.

Body-Image Blues

Surprisingly, a woman's actual physical attractiveness has little to do with how she feels about herself or her body. The diagram below shows the relationship between physical beauty, self-worth and body image.

Beauty-Worth-Image-Relationship

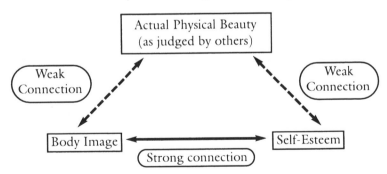

The connection is weak between how attractive we actually are as rated by other people and our body image. Nor is there much connection between our actual attractiveness and self-worth. A woman can be considered beautiful and feel ugly, or she can be considered unattractive and feel confident in her body image. However, there is a strong link between a woman's body image and her feeling of self-worth. When a woman has a bad body image, she tends to have low self-esteem. On the other hand, a woman who has higher self-esteem views her body more favorably regardless of her looks. Even when a woman's body image is inaccurate, it serves as subjective reality. If she thinks her hips are too big or her nose is huge, then that is projected to her as reality and it affects her self-worth negatively.[8] We can see, then, how important it is to develop healthy attitudes regarding our self-esteem and body image.

Childhood Images

Parents play a crucial role in shaping their daughter's self-image. Many attitudes about self-image are formed in childhood. In a *Family Circle* poll, daughters who considered themselves unattractive were more likely to have overly critical mothers or silent fathers who said nothing about them at all. It seems that the lack of praise can be just as bad as constant criticism.[9]

Some women recall childhoods full of family ridicule. They internalize negative labels such as "klutz," "fatso" and "four eyes" that they can never quite escape. One mother told her daughter she had better be smart because she was too ugly to attract a husband on her looks alone.

Other women were praised so much for their looks as children that they believe their self-worth is dependent on that single aspect of their lives. They feel self-conscious and burdened always to be "Momma and Daddy's Pretty Baby." Their parents overinvested in their child's looks instead of helping her develop her whole self.[10]

Developing the whole self is especially important during the teen years because adolescence can have a tremendous impact on a girl's fragile body image. Teens are greatly influenced by the media, which sets unrealistic standards. One study showed that female adolescents were "significantly more troubled than boys, with anxiety over appearance the major cause; twice as many girls as boys attempt suicide."[11]

Mary Pipher, in her book *Reviving Ophelia*, tells how Maria, an Hispanic teenager, worked to develop a healthy self-image despite society's conflicting messages. Maria said,

> I tacked up a list of positives about myself on the mirror. I asked myself at the end of each day what I had done that I felt proud of. That work on self-esteem helped in junior high. When I felt badly because my body wasn't perfect, I remembered my suggestions to think positively.[12]

Reshaping Our Body Image

In reshaping the way we see our body, we all need the positive reinforcement of praise – even from ourselves. By writing down 10 meaningful compliments that we genuinely believe about our bodies, we can use them as a weapon to combat our own negative self-talk or thoughts about ourselves. For instance, when you tell yourself a downer like, "My hands look awful," replace it with a neutral or positive statement like, "I'm disturbed about my hands," or "My hands usually look better than this." Reframing our critical statements helps us put them in a more realistic perspective.

Often we as Christians think we might seem conceited or proud if we accept compliments from other people or even ourselves. Does humility mean constantly debasing ourselves? No, we can still be humble and have a healthy self-concept without downgrading ourselves. Jesus said that the greatest commandment is to love God, but the next greatest commandment is to love our neighbor as ourselves. He assumed that before we can love another, we first must have a healthy respect and love for ourselves (Matthew 22:37-39).

We need to learn to accept compliments graciously by saying, "Thank you." If we negate a compliment, we not only put ourselves down but also insult the opinion of the complimenter. Accepting compliments on our looks is a part of accepting ourselves. Teri Twitty-Villani writes, "Accepting yourself for who you are adds more to your physical beauty than all the clothes and makeup in the world."[13]

Exercise can make us feel good about our bodies. We don't have to be fitness freaks. Just find a sport or exercise that's fun and invest your wholehearted energy into it. Whether or not you lose weight or change your shape, you will feel better about your body.

The mirror doesn't have to be our enemy. Some women go to the extreme of never looking in mirrors for fear of what they will see. Other women check every few minutes to see if their hair or makeup is out of place. In both cases, mirrors have become more of a trap than an aid. Use your mirror to affirm your looks. Improve what you can – then go on with your life. Remember Erma Bombeck's daily declaration: "I'm me and I'm wonderful. Because God doesn't make junk."[14]

Knowing that Jesus accepts us makes it easier to accept ourselves. Jill Briscoe writes, "Coming to know God in Christ helps us to realize someone loves us just the way we are. He likes our height, hair, and even our particular personality. ... As you get to love Him who patterns you, you actually get to love and accept the pattern!"[15]

Toward Born-Again Beauty

God and society use very different measures for judging beauty. This contrast is clearly seen in the choosing of Israel's first two kings. After hearing Israel's desire to have a king like other nations, God sends Samuel to anoint Saul, "an impressive young man without equal among the Israelites – a head taller than any of the others" (1 Samuel 9:2). Saul must have stood out in a crowd! But his heart didn't stay true to the Lord, and another king was chosen.

The new king, David, was good-looking, but, more importantly, he was a man after God's own heart. When Samuel was ready to anoint David's older brother, Eliab, as the new king, God reminded the prophet, "Do not consider his appearance or his height, for I have rejected him. The LORD does not look at things man looks at. Man looks at the outward appearance, but the LORD looks at the heart" (16:7).

God is more concerned about our hearts than about how the world views our bodies. He focuses on what a woman is made of, not on her makeup. How refreshing to know that although our bodies grow old, we can be renewed constantly in God's eyes through His Word. We can be born of God with a born-again beauty that only He can bestow. Peter tells Christians, "For you have been born again, not of perishable seed, but of imperishable, through the living and enduring word of God" (1 Peter 1:23). Whether we are born beautiful or not, we can all glow with a born-again beauty from God!

Inside Out

1. Why do you think one study found that American women had more negative feelings about their bodies than women in any other culture studied?

2. What is the relationship between self-worth, body image and actual physical beauty as shown in the diagram in this chapter?

3. How can families affect children's self-image by their criticism and praise?

4. What are some ways we can reshape our body image?

5. How can we accept a compliment graciously without becoming conceited?

6. How did Saul demonstrate his low self-esteem when Samuel chose him among the people (1 Samuel 10:21-22)? (It was not easy because he was so tall!)

7. Describe the outer appearances of Saul and David at their anointings. What did God look at when He chose David and rejected Saul?

8. Contrast the physical birth with the spiritual birth that Jesus discusses with Nicodemus in John 3:1-8.

9. What is the washing of "rebirth and renewal by the Holy Spirit" that Paul writes about in Titus 3:5?

10. What are some characteristics of the children born of God from these scriptures in 1 John: 2:29; 3:9; 4:7; 5:1, 4, 18?

The Way It Was

A JEWISH LAUNDRY

With their garments woven by hand, women in Bible times had to wash and take care of what they had. They tried to do their laundry in running water, sometimes using a detergent called *borit*. This probably was a lye, but it is often translated "soap" (Malachi 3:2). No doubt it was hard on the hands.[16]

The wealthy had slaves to wash their clothes, or they could send them to a fuller. A fuller was not a traveling brush salesman, as we might think today, but a laundry man who stomped out grime with his feet in copper tubs or beat the cloth with sticks and spread out the garments to dry.[17]

The fuller's soap could contain alkaline, soda, potash and herbs. Because of the offensive smell, the fuller usually was stationed outside the city walls. In Jerusalem the fuller worked outside the east wall in a fuller's or "Washerman's Field," where a conduit for water and a highway passed through (2 Kings 18:17; Isaiah 7:3; 36:2).

Fullers discovered a way to bleach cloth white. The fullers' bleach consisted of a mixture of putrid urine, alkali, soap, fumes of sulfur, and ashes of certain desert plants.[18] No matter how hard they tried, however, they could never bleach clothes as "dazzling white" as the garments of Jesus when He was transfigured in Mark 9:3.

Chapter 5

$\mathcal{T}$HE GOOD, THE BAD AND THE BEAUTIFUL

"We can declare that because we are fashioned by God, we are beautiful."

Judith Couchman[1]

$\mathcal{S}$TOP FOR A MOMENT and close your eyes. Visualize in your mind's eye what you think Abraham's wife Sarah looked like. How about Ruth or Bathsheba or Mary or Martha or Priscilla or Phoebe? In some instances the Bible gives us clues about how these women looked, but in other cases it remains silent. Let's look at how physical beauty affected some women in the Bible.

Beauty in the Old Testament

The first biblical reference to female physical beauty occurs in Genesis 6:2, which describes how the sons of God saw that the daughters of men were beautiful and married them. Many scholars think this was the first intermarriage between followers of God and unbelievers.[2] Here the beauty of women became a snare to tempt good men to go astray. The end result was wickedness so great that God sent a flood to cleanse the Earth and start all over.

Later we read about beauty to lie for (Genesis 12:10-20). When Abram journeyed to Egypt to escape a famine, he feared that the

Egyptians would see his wife's beauty and kill him. Abram told Sarai, who was both his wife and half sister, to say only that she was his sister. Pharaoh's officials saw her beauty, and Sarai was taken into Pharaoh's palace. Rather than killing Abram, Pharaoh treated him well for Sarai's sake. The deception seemed to work. But soon the royal household was inflicted with serious diseases. When Pharaoh found out the cause – Abram and Sarai's lie – he sent them away from Egypt. Sarai's beauty had been used for deceit.

Abraham and Sarah didn't learn from their experience. A similar scenario occurred with Abimelech, king of Gerar (Genesis 20). Fortunately God intervened in a dream before Sarah and Abimelech's marriage was consummated. Until Sarah was returned to Abraham, none of the women in Abimelech's household could bear children. Even Isaac, Abraham's son, spread a similar lie with King Abimelech about his beautiful wife Rebekah (24:16; 26:1-11).

God did not direct Abraham and Isaac to lie. Their own lack of faith was the problem. Physical loveliness was involved in these deceptions. A wife's beauty actually became a problem for her husband in these cases.

Another wife's beauty was instrumental in her husband's death. At a time when kings went off to war, King David was fighting a battle at home – temptation. He saw the beautiful Bathsheba bathing, had her brought to the palace for his pleasure, and Bathsheba became pregnant. David, trying to hide their sin, ordered her husband, Uriah, be put in the forefront of the battle where he would be killed. Bathsheba then became David's wife (2 Samuel 11). Their child died as a consequence of their sin.

In these instances, beauty led men down the path of sin. Although being beautiful is not bad in itself, it can have bad effects. Does this mean we should put sacks over our heads and start thinking that the only way to be holy is to be homely? Fortunately, no.

The Good and the Beautiful

We have several examples of women in the Old Testament who were good and beautiful. Abigail was blessed with beauty and wisdom. The story in 1 Samuel 25 tells how she was married to the rich but surly Nabal, who refused to share his bounty at sheepshearing time with David and his tired, famished troops. When

David remembered how he had protected Nabal's shepherds and flocks when they were nearby, he grew angry at Nabal's lack of hospitality. "Put on your swords!" David commanded his 400-strong army and headed off to kill all the males of Nabal's household. Fortunately, a servant informed Abigail of their impending doom. She quickly prepared a massive order of bread, wine, sheep, grain, raisins and figs and loaded them on donkeys. When she met David on the road, she bowed low and took the blame for not seeing David's men when they came to ask for provisions. David was probably as impressed by her quick thinking as much as her beauty. Nabal died from heart failure when he learned what Abigail had done, and David sent for her to become his wife and, later, his queen.

Another woman became a queen after spending a year in beauty treatments – six months each of regimens with oil of myrrh, perfumes and cosmetics and with special food, too. The Bible says Esther was "lovely in form and features" (Esther 2:7). She was taken to King Xerxes' palace after he dethroned Queen Vashti. There, with all the other beauties in the kingdom, Esther was primped and primed for a beauty contest of royal proportions with all the other virgins. She won the heart of the king and became his queen.

This sounds almost like a Cinderella tale, but evil was also at work. Mordecai, Esther's adoptive father, refused to bow down before Haman, a royal official of Xerxes. Haman devised a plan to annihilate Mordecai and the entire Jewish nation. However, there was a problem Haman was unaware of – Esther was also a Jew.

With the encouragement of Mordecai, Esther interceded with Xerxes in an attempt to save the Jewish people and herself. She went before the seemingly unapproachable king and, in a series of banquets, exposed Haman and his evil scheme. In the end, Haman was hanged on the gallows intended for Mordecai, and Xerxes ordered that the Jews be spared.

Although God's name is not mentioned in the book of Esther, His providence is certainly seen in the saving of the Jews. Esther was put where she was for a purpose. Mordecai realized this when he said, "And who knows but that you have come to royal position for such a time as this?" (4:14). How did she initially get there? God used Esther's beauty to bring her into a place of authority to save His people.

One book in the Bible has more references to physical beauty than any other. The Song of Solomon is definitely unique for its frank account of human love. Some scholars believe that this book symbolically illustrates the great love God has for the church, as a husband has for his wife (Isaiah 54:4-6; Ephesians 5:21-33).

Other scholars say the Song of Solomon is an account of Solomon's romance with a beautiful country shepherdess whom he wooed in the garb of a shepherd. Solomon possibly took time off from his official duties to vacation in the country. He took her to the palace in Jerusalem to be his wife. Unfortunately she became one of many wives, and this episode was followed by many others. Gleason L. Archer says it well:

> The Song of Solomon serves as a reminder to all believers that God rejoices in His handiwork and knows how to invest it with thrilling beauty that deserves a full and proper appreciation. Yet along with this warm response to all that God has made beautiful – whether landscape, sky, sea, the magnificent trees, gorgeous flowers, or the transient charms of human loveliness – we must never forget to give all the glory and worship to the One who fashioned them so. We must always remember to exalt the Creator above all His creation and above all His creatures.[3]

New Testament Beauty

The New Testament says very little about physical attractiveness. In fact, not one woman's looks are described in the entire New Testament! God, knowing how transient and fading external beauty is, must have wanted us to focus on the inner beauty of the Spirit.

The few references to beauty in the New Testament are quite enlightening. In showing how a Christian wife can win her nonbelieving husband to Christ by actions rather than words, Peter states:

> Your beauty should not come from outward adornment, such as braided hair and the wearing of gold jewelry and fine clothes. Instead, it should be that of your inner self, the unfading beau-

ty of a gentle and quiet spirit, which is of great worth in God's sight (1 Peter 3:3-4).

Does this mean that we should make no effort to beautify ourselves outwardly? Is it wrong to wear braided hair, gold jewelry or fine clothes? A close examination of the passage shows that this verse is overstatement for effect, a Hebraism, that is, a common form of exhortation in sacred writing that should not be taken literally. Another example of this kind of Hebraism is John 6:27: "Do not work for food that spoils, but for food that endures to eternal life." Jesus is not saying, "Don't work at all," but "Put your priority on eternal nourishment from God."[4]

In the same way, Peter says that a woman should make inner beauty her priority. He later states that it was inner loveliness that made the holy women of the past beautiful. He singles out Sarah, noting how she submitted to her husband, Abraham, and how we become her daughters when we "do what is right and do not give way to fear" (1 Peter 3:6). Although Sarah's physical beauty caused her some problems, here she is praised for her inward beauty, specifically her submissive attitude.

Similarly Paul writes:

> I also want women to dress modestly, with decency and propriety, not with braided hair or gold or pearls or expensive clothes, but with good deeds, appropriate for women who profess to worship God (1 Timothy 2:9-10).

In Paul's day wealthy women sat for hours while their servants plaited and curled their hair, often into fancy shapes. Then their hair was secured by pearl nets, gold pins, tortoise-shell or ivory combs, or jewel-studded headbands that drew attention by glistening in the light.[5] Some would spend exorbitant amounts of money on their jewels and clothes. Peter and Paul condemn this excessive behavior.

So the true Christian woman is not destined to become a card-carrying member of the Slob Squad. Peter and Paul do not advocate neglecting our outward appearance but rather instruct us to put the emphasis on our inward grooming. We should spend most of our time, money and effort developing our inner "loveliness." The unfading beauty of a gentle and quiet spirit is a loveliness that every woman can achieve with the Lord's help. Only God can take us as we are – the good and the bad – and make us beautiful.

Inside Out

1. What part, if any, did beauty play in these beautiful women's lives?
   * Tamar, Absalom's sister (2 Samuel 13:1)
   * Tamar, Absalom's daughter (2 Samuel 14:27)
   * Abishag (1 Kings 1:3-4)
   * Daughters of Job (Job 42:15)

2. In Galatians 2:6 how does Paul say that God judges?

3. How did Jesus warn that looks could be deceiving in Matthew 23:27-28?

4. Who has beautiful feet (Isaiah 52:7; Romans 10:15)? Why do you think this symbolism is used?

5. How does Proverbs 6:24-29 show that a wicked woman's beauty can be used as an enticement for evil?

6. How did physical beauty positively and negatively affect events in these women's lives: Sarah, Rebekah, Bathsheba, Abigail and Esther?

7. What are possible explanations for understanding the emotional meaning of the Song of Solomon?

8. Why do you think that no woman's physical appearance is mentioned in the New Testament?

9. Define the Hebraism of overstatement and give an example.

10. From where should a Christian woman's real beauty come (1 Peter 3:3-4)? Does this mean that Peter condones neglecting our outward appearance?

*B*ATHING

*W*hat a treat it is to escape our troubles in a soothing bath! Since antiquity, bathing has been a relaxing, luxurious time for the privileged. But this was not always a possibility for the majority of people. Many people had neither the water nor the desire to bathe.[6] The rich in biblical times might have had bathrooms, but more likely they bathed in springs or rivers like Pharaoh's daughter (Exodus 2:5). Later, Greek and Roman baths provided public places for bathing. During the years of King Ahab's rule, there might have been a public pool in Samaria where the prostitutes bathed (1 Kings 22:38), but most Hebrews bathed in private.[7]

The bathing we read about in the Bible often meant a partial bath consisting of washing the feet in a small earthenware bowl. It typically took place in the evening after the day's activities.[8] Dusty roads made it necessary to wash one's feet frequently, and foot washing was a custom when visiting in someone's home (Genesis 18:4; 19:2). It is easier to understand why Jesus said, as He washed the disciples' feet, "A person who has had a bath needs only to wash his feet: his whole body is clean" (John 13:10).

Under Old Testament worship, bathing served as a ritual act of purification from ceremonial defilement caused by contact with the dead or defiled persons or things (Leviticus 14:8-9; 15:5-27; 17:15-16).[9] A worshiper could not approach the altar until he had bathed in running water and washed his clothes (15:13). This practice was for hygienic purposes as well as reverence for God.[10]

Chapter 6

THE SEARCH FOR REAL BEAUTY

"Sadly, after centuries of pursuing the fleeting and physical, as a culture we've buried our innate need for spiritual treasures under a pile of costumes and cosmetics, diets and disciplines."

Judith Couchman[1]

THE NEXT TIME you go to the grocery store, look at the magazines as you check out. Take a mental count of ones with beautiful models gracing the covers and featuring topics concerning beauty – makeovers, diet, hairstyles or sex appeal. We just can't seem to get enough of beauty topics or "beauty-speak."

Looking good is obviously important, but how did we become so obsessed with looks? Learning about mankind's perceptions of beauty in the past and contrasting that with the light of God's Word will help us better understand our attitudes today.

Beauty in Ancient Times

Have you ever wondered when women first began to desire to be pretty? Perhaps it happened when one saw her reflection in a pool of water. Can you picture her catching a glimpse of herself and sighing, "Oh, no, another bad hair day!"

We do know that in early civilizations, women used whatever means they had to improve their physical beauty. During the time of Abraham, women in Mesopotamia already used various forms of makeup. Living in this culture, Sarah might have used black mineral pastes to paint her eyes and eyebrows. Originally this was probably done to protect the eyes from the bright sunlight (like football players), but soon it became fashionable in Mesopotamia, Palestine and Egypt. This eye paint, a paste made from mixing ground powder and gum or water, was kept in a receptacle and applied with a spatula.[2] Visualize a woman utilizing her beauty aids:

They even sent messages for men who came from far away, and when they arrived you bathed yourself for them, painted your eyes and put on your jewelry. You sat on an elegant couch, with a table spread before it on which you had placed the incense and oil that belonged to me (Ezekiel 23:40-41).

The Lord is speaking symbolically of the adulterous nation of Israel, but the description holds true for the beauty regimen of some women of that time. Even more descriptive is Isaiah 3:16-24:

The Lord says, "The women of Zion are haughty, walking along with outstretched necks, flirting with their eyes, tripping along with mincing steps, with ornaments jingling on their ankles. Therefore the Lord will bring sores on the heads of the women of Zion; the Lord will make their scalps bald." In that day the Lord will snatch away their finery: the bangles and headbands and crescent necklaces, the earrings and bracelets and veils, the headdresses and ankle chains and sashes, the perfume bottles and charms, the signet rings and nose rings, the fine robes and the capes and cloaks, the purses and mirrors, and the linen garments and tiaras and shawls. Instead of fragrance there will be a stench; instead of a sash, a rope; instead of well-dressed hair, baldness; instead of fine clothing, sackcloth; instead of beauty, branding.

Isaiah presents a graphic contrast between the efforts of Zion's women to make themselves beautiful and the calamity to come when Judah and Jerusalem would be overtaken by their Babylonian enemies. However, the passage also gives interesting details on jewelry, clothing and other beauty aids of the time.

Centuries later the Greeks, and eventually the Romans, came to power. Perceptions of beauty were greatly influenced by these two cultures. The Greeks glorified the human body, primarily the male; male beauty contests were held for the enjoyment of men. But the Greeks believed one should ultimately aspire to the divine beauty of the Greek gods, which took the best features from different humans. The Romans thought that physical beauty in women was something for men to admire. They applauded female performers in scant "bikinis," for example![3] Sexual beauty was an important part of worship to many of their goddesses.

Fairy Tales and Reality

Beautiful women have been the inspiration for art and literature throughout the centuries. Conversely, ugliness has been associated with evil. Often, deformed women were thought to be witches. One only needs to reread a few fairy tales – *Beauty and the Beast, Sleeping Beauty, Snow White* or *Cinderella* – to verify this.[4]

In reality, most common people were too busy scratching a living from the land to worry about looks. The British historian Arthur Marwick writes:

> They were mobile neither geographically nor socially: the peasant lived, worked, married and died within his own community. For neither man nor woman was there much choice in the way of sexual partners: the notion of choosing someone because of their superior personal appearance was an almost meaningless one. Standards of nutrition and health were low and so also, therefore, were sex drives: marriage was overwhelmingly a matter of stern practicality rather than of sexual gratification. Again, therefore, personal appearance was scarcely a matter of great concern. ... Even for the highest born, life was brutish and potentially short: every sinew had to be stretched towards maintaining and, if possible, improving the family fortunes.[5]

As society became more urbanized and mobile, more choices and comparisons could be made between the sexes. With the Renaissance came humanist ideas like that of Lorenzo Valla in 1430: "Pleasure is the true good ... what is sweeter, what more delectable, what more adorable, than a fair face?"[6] He recommended that beautiful women should wear as little as possible in the summer. Eventually the idea of personal appearance became separated from ideas of goodness or religious moralizing. Artists attempted to capture the beauty of women on canvas as they saw it.[7]

However, no matter what the philosophers or painters thought, keeping alive was far more important than keeping beautiful. Historian Charles Perron cited two sayings of that day: "You can't eat beauty with a spoon" and "When one has a beautiful wife, one has no fine pigs – why? Because the pigs, instead of eating, spend all their time staring at her."[8] Another historian, Edward Shorter, writes that the peasants of Baden, Germany, warned, "Look at the money bag not at the face."[9]

Even people in the upper classes, who had more of a choice in marriage, often married for status or wealth. Compatibility was seen to be more important than physical attractiveness. Health was another consideration. A robust wife bore children, who in turn continued the blood line and provided labor and help in old age. With poor living standards and rampant disease, it was rare for a man or woman not be be cursed with malnutrition, pockmarks or congenital defects.

Cultivating beauty, however, became more and more important as economic and living conditions improved. In the 19th century, women dressed up in colorful, elaborate and sometimes extravagant outfits, while men wore more sober apparel. Judging by their clothes, it seemed that a woman's place was to dress up and be beautiful, while a man's role was one of hard work and respectability.[10]

After the 1860s, increased travel opportunities and expansion of the printing industry gave more people the ability to see, compare and contrast beauty. Previously, they only had drawings or paintings; now they had photographs of famous beauties like Sarah Bernhardt. No matter how women might hide themselves under crinolines and bonnets, men were viewing new standards of beauty daily in books and newspapers.[11]

The 20th century brought a myriad of changes in attitudes toward beauty. The World Wars disrupted traditional ways of life. With the horrors of war, some people lost their faith in God. As morals were loosened, sex became closely associated with beauty. The popularity of film and TV stars reached new heights with exposure through magazines and fan clubs. These stars set the standards for beauty, and because of their success and lavish lifestyles, they were labeled "beautiful people." Models became millionaires just on their looks. Beauty could sell – and do it quite well.[12]

Will the Real Beauty Stand Up?

People have tried to find real beauty throughout the ages, but it has been an elusive search. Standards have been set by cultural definitions of beauty. The seekers of beauty have searched in vain because they were looking in the wrong places.

Where is true beauty? Only in Jesus Christ and those remade in His image! Real beauty is not dependent on our outward decoration, but on our inner declaration that Jesus is Lord. Our real beauty comes through our joy of salvation through Jesus. Zechariah 9:16-17 proclaims, "The LORD their God will save them on that day as the flock of his people. They will sparkle in his land like jewels in a crown. How attractive and beautiful they will be!"

Inside Out

1. Name some ancient jewelry, clothes and beauty aids mentioned in Isaiah 3:16-24.

2. With the Greek and Roman emphasis on bodily development, what did Paul write Timothy regarding the physical training of the body (1 Timothy 4:7-8)?

3. Contrast how religious leaders and artists/writers saw beautiful women in medieval times.

4. Until the late 19th century, why did looks not play a crucial part in the selection of a mate? What were important factors to consider in marriage at that time?

5. After the 1860s, what better enabled people to see and compare beautiful women?

6. What changes in attitudes toward beauty occurred in the 20th century?

7. What woman did Joab tell not to put on her "cosmetic lotions" in her pretense of mourning before King David (2 Samuel 14:2)?

8. What cosmetic is mentioned in Jeremiah 4:30?

9. What bejeweled animal is compared to a beautiful woman without discretion (Proverbs 11:22)?

$\mathcal{S}$ANDALS AND SHOES

*N*ot all of us have 3,000 pairs of shoes like Imelda Marcos, but we usually have a closetful.[13] Women in Bible times were lucky to have two pairs. The poor usually went barefoot.[14] At that time shoes were made of soft leather and shaped like boots. Sandals, designed for rougher wear, were made of a harder leather nailed to soles of cane, wood or palm tree bark. They were fastened by thongs (Genesis 14:23) and could be patched for longer use (Joshua 9:5). The well-dressed woman in Ezekiel 16:10 wore leather sandals with her embroidered dress.[15]

Some of us like to kick off our shoes for comfort, but ancient people removed their shoes for many reasons. Shoes were taken off before entering the house to prevent tracking in dirt from the unpaved streets as a sign of respect and consideration.[16] Shoes were also removed when approaching God (Exodus 3:5; Joshua 5:15) and when mourning (2 Samuel 15:30).[17]

Shoes also played a part in "levirate" marriages. If a man refused to fulfill his responsibility by marrying his brother's widow, the widow went before the town elders, took one of the man's sandals, and spit in his face! His family line would be called The Family of the Unsandaled (Deuteronomy 25:5-10).[18]

The shoe was considered the lowliest piece of apparel in Bible times, so we can better understand the indignation of Amos over the haughty practice of selling the poor for the price of sandals (Amos 8:6). We also can see the humility of John the Baptist in saying that he would be unworthy even to stoop down and untie the sandals of the Son of God (Mark 1:7).

Chapter 7

*E*SCAPING THE COMPETITION TRAP

"Whatever we may buy to please ourselves – cars, houses, vacations – we buy beauty with more desperation, investing in its power because of the gnawing envy we feel when we see beauty in others."

Nancy Friday[1]

*W*EDDING NIGHTS are often full of surprises, but few husbands are as surprised as newlywed Jacob on the morning after. Fully intending to see his love Rachel in the light of day, he finds instead that her older sister Leah had spent the night in his arms. Jacob had worked seven years for Rachel, the woman he loved, and now had to work seven more to secure her – ending up with two wives. The devious plan of Rachel and Leah's father Laban spawned a complex competition between the two women.

The Bible contrasts the two sisters in Genesis 29:17: "Leah had weak eyes, but Rachel was lovely in form, and beautiful." "Weak eyes" did not necessarily imply that Leah had defective vision; her eyes may have lacked the luster and brilliance that Eastern peoples admired.[2] Perhaps "it may mean that her only beauty lay in the softness of her eyes, whereas Rachel was a beauty from head to toe."[3] Was Leah envious of Rachel's looks or of Jacob's apparent feelings for her sister? Whatever the reason, the conflict between them continued even after they became Jacob's wives.

Leah soon found a contest with Rachel she could win – bearing children. Leah might not win Jacob's love, but she could have his children. In fact, Rachel became so jealous of Leah that she demanded of Jacob, " 'Give me children, or I'll die!' Jacob became angry with her and said, 'Am I in the place of God, who has kept you from having children?' " (Genesis 30:1-2). Rachel then suggested that Jacob have children through her servant Bilhah. When Bilhah bore Jacob two sons, Rachel seemingly tasted victory and said, "I have had a great struggle with my sister, and I have won" (v. 8). Leah responded by giving her maidservant Zilpah to Jacob for a wife.

Here we see competition – that may have lasted the rest of their lives – between women over looks, children and the affection of their shared husband. It made both players miserable.

Although Rachel and Leah's conflict occurred a long time ago, are we really so different today? Ironically, *Working Woman* magazine heralded the new trademark of today's woman – a competitive spirit.[4] The world says that a contemporary woman can have it all if she competes for it. Perhaps the arenas have changed, but competition between women is nothing new. One of the most common areas of conflict is beauty.

The Daily Beauty Contest

We've probably all felt it – that twinge of jealousy when a truly gorgeous woman enters the room. Some women even have their own rating system for the way other women look. If the woman looks too good, other women often resent her. If she looks bad, they dismiss her. It's almost as if they secretly distrust the other woman, even if they know nothing about her. Naomi Wolf writes, "Beauty thinking teaches women to be enemies until they know they are friends."[5] Studies have found that we choose to see and judge people by what is most important and sensitive to us, like weight, complexion or height.[6]

We are also bombarded by the media's ideal of beauty, which causes a type of envy. Consider women's beauty magazines, for example. Why are they filled with seminude women selling everything from perfume to underwear, all aimed at women? Do we sometimes yearn to have bodies just like the models?

A prime example of this lure of the media is the *Sports Illustrated* swimsuit issue, known for scantily clad bathing beauties in tropical locales. This issue attracts men and women in its readership. In fact, sales triple among women for this issue. Do women want to look only at the new spring swimsuits? They may not unabashedly pore over the issue the same way men do, but they can fantasize about possessing the models' beauty.

Debra Evans writes:

> Today's beauty industry exploits and manipulates women's tendency toward covetousness and envy of beauty just as the international pornography industry exploits and manipulates men's visual tendency toward sexual lust. For too long, we've focused on keeping *Playboy* and *Penthouse* out of our homes for the sake of our men without seriously considering the effect distorted beauty ideals have on us. ... While we're understandably outraged by the pornography epidemic, the allure of beauty offers a much more subtle brand of temptation for women.[7]

The competition for beauty can entrap us in other ways. Some women try to out-diet each other, seeing who can be the thinnest or eat the least. They compete for men by trying to look the youngest or the prettiest. Often mother-daughter and sister-sister conflicts arise over looks, sometimes unconsciously. Other women are such perfectionists that they constantly try to meet an unrealistic ideal. They never feel satisfied with what they do or how they look. They keep detailed charts of weight and diet, weigh themselves before and after meals, and never think they measure up.[8]

Beyond Competition

The trouble with the competition trap is that no matter how hard we try, we really can't win. Someone else is always around to compete against. The conflict is neverending. We will probably end up either thinking we are not good enough (self-depreciation) or thinking we are better than other people (conceit). Paul urges,

> Let us not become conceited, provoking and envying each other. ... If anyone thinks he is something when he is noth-

ing, he deceives himself. Each one should test his own actions. Then he can take pride in himself, without comparing himself to somebody else (Galatians 5:26; 6:3-4).

We each have a responsibility to do the best we reasonably can so that we can have a healthy self-image, not conceited pride. But if we are always worrying about how we rate in comparison with other people, then we will become self-absorbed with little thought for anyone else. An unknown sage has quipped, "Every time we turn green with envy we are ripe for trouble."[9]

Paul says it is not wise to classify or compare ourselves with other people (2 Corinthians 10:12). We should guard against loaded expressions of comparison – "er" statements (She's heavier, taller, prettier); "too" statements (I'm too skinny, my nose is too big); and "as/as" comparisons (My feet aren't as big as Miss Bigfeet's).[10]

Again Paul exhorts, "Do not think of yourself more highly than you ought, but rather think of yourself with sober judgment, in accordance with the measure of faith God has given you" (Romans 12:3). He then explains that each church member has a unique capacity to serve, just as each part of the human body performs a function. We have no reason to compete because we each have different gifts to give and individual ways to serve (1 Corinthians 12:12-31). We can accept each other, unique as we are, because Christ first accepted us (Romans 15:7).

In this dog-eat-dog world, Paul's words to Timothy sound even sweeter: "But godliness with contentment is great gain" (1 Timothy 6:6). Contentment is a lost art and a forgotten attitude, but it is never too late to start developing the trait. Being content doesn't justify becoming a slob, but rather accepting what we are, how we look, and what we can achieve through our Lord. "I have learned to be content whatever the circumstances. ... I can do everything through him who gives me strength" (Philippians 4:11, 13).

Developing multiple talents and interests is one way to live beyond competition. The more dimensions we have, the healthier our self-image and the more difficult it is for a setback in one area to devastate us completely. If something makes us feel less attractive, we can look to other areas of competence that are not so closely tied to looks. God has given us many qualities and abilities that we can use for Him; why limit ourselves or His power?

Think of the many roles of the virtuous woman in Proverbs 31. She had a multitude of interests and abilities and was praised for her efforts. In the total sphere of a vibrant, righteous woman's life, beauty and charm are shown to be transient and of less importance than ability and spiritual qualities. What really makes a woman worthy – her life or her looks? The writer leaves no doubt that it is the active, God-fearing woman who is blessed (v. 30).

Another way to escape the competition trap is to avoid situations where beauty comparisons are often made. That isn't always easy when family or work climates are primed for this kind of thinking. Friends have a powerful influence, so choose friends who have many interests and aren't consumed with beauty and shopping. One study found that girls joining sororities at the University of Michigan absorbed the same feelings about thinness as the group held. In fact, the new recruits wanted to outdo them.[11] These young women needed to find the right kinds of models.

Finding the Right Model

Unless we exist alone on a desert island, we will see other women. But we don't have to be ensnared by the competition trap. It doesn't matter whether the competition comes from our next door neighbor or an international model, it's a no-win situation. We need to look beyond human models to Jesus. "Do nothing out of selfish ambition or vain conceit, but in humility consider others better than yourselves. Each of you should look not only to your own interests, but also to the interests of others. Your attitude should be the same as that of Christ Jesus" (Philippians 2:3-6).

Where can we find the perfect model to emulate without feeling either superior or put down? Where can we find a compassionate friend who wants us to win the prize of eternity without having to compete against anyone else for it? Who loves us when we look beautiful and when we don't? Jesus! Will we be frustrated, always comparing our sinful selves to this perfect model? We could, but with Him, there is clearly no competition!

Inside Out

1. What might have been some reasons for the competition between Rachel and Leah? What part did mandrakes play in their rivalry (Genesis 30:14-16)?

2. What beautiful woman besides Rachel was jealous of another younger woman (Genesis 16; 21:8-21)?

3. Is there a difference between jealousy and envy?

4. What did the wise man in Ecclesiastes 4:4 say motivates all labor and all achievement? How does this relate to us today?

5. What are some ways competition for beauty can entrap women today?

6. How can we take pride in ourselves without becoming conceited (Galatians 5:26; 6:3-4)?

7. List the many roles of the virtuous woman in Proverbs 31. How do women's roles compare today?

8. How can developing different gifts give a woman less reason to feel the need to compete for beauty?

9. In finding the right model, who or what does the writer say to imitate?

   a. 1 Corinthians 4:16

   b. Hebrews 6:12

   c. Hebrews 13:7

   d. 3 John 11

10. Paul tells the Thessalonians they should be imitators of whom? Who became the models?

    a. 1 Thessalonians 1:6-7

    b. 1 Thessalonians 2:14; 2 Thessalonians 3:9

The Way It Was

NOSE RINGS AND ARM BRACELETS

A nose ring, arm bracelets, gold and silver jewelry and nice clothes – how's that for gifts to start off a prospective male-female relationship? These are the gifts Abraham's servant gave Rebekah when he was sent to find a wife for Isaac. In fact, Rebekah has the distinction of being the first bejeweled woman we read of in the Bible (Genesis 24:47, 53).

In his prophecy against the king of Tyre, Ezekiel enumerates the array of jewels at that time: "[E]very precious stone adorned you: ruby, topaz and emerald, chrysolite, onyx and jasper, sapphire, turquoise and beryl. Your settings and mountings were made of gold" (Ezekiel 28:13). Later, during the days of the Roman Empire, women wore the most luxurious jewels they could afford, such as diamonds from India and pearls from the oyster beds of the Indian Ocean, Arabian coast and Persian Gulf.[12]

Jewelry was popular with women in Bible times (Exodus 35:22; Song of Solomon 1:10-11; Ezekiel 16:11-13; Hosea 2:13). There were bracelets, anklets, necklaces, diadems, finger rings, pendants, jeweled perfume and ointment boxes, crescents for camels, gems for head attire, amulets and pendants with magical meanings, and gold nets for the hair. These accessories could be acquired through betrothals, personal gifts or spoils of war.

Every king had a goldsmith, and most large cities had silver-smiths.[13] Most poor people could not afford jewelry, but the rich often went to extravagant measures in their purchases. The Roman writer Seneca complained that Roman women wore the value of two or three estates with a single earring.[14]

Chapter 8

PAYING THE PRICE FOR VANITY

"Every man at his best state is altogether vanity."

(Psalm 39:5 KJV)

IN 1990, MAGAZINE EDITOR Charla Krupp spent $7,398 beautifying her body, face and hair. Although the New Yorker admits giving the "college tuition of her unborn child" to her hairdresser, she says she isn't the highest-maintenance person she knows. With expenses like health club yearly dues at $1,298, every-other-week $30 massages, and an $80 facial every three months, she explains:

> Being a high-maintenance woman isn't for everyone. It takes an enormous amount of time, an endless supply of funds and relentless dedication to the cause of self-improvement. I don't have a hobby, so I guess this is mine. Who can put a price tag on that fabulous glow you get when you're your thinnest, your blondest, your pores their tiniest, and every inch of you is waxed all shiny and new? Certainly not I.[1]

What price tag do *we* put on beautifying ourselves? How much time, money and effort do we spend? When is the cost too great for us as

Christian women? To some women, the pursuit of loveliness is so important that they are willing to do almost anything they can to achieve it. Let's look at a queen whose vanity reached royal proportions.

Gone to the Dogs

Few names are as notorious as Jezebel. From 1 Kings 17 through 2 Kings 9, we read about this idolatrous wife of Ahab, king of Israel. She was the epitome of evil and proud of it. Jezebel played a crucial role in leading her husband and the nation into Baal worship. She also opposed Elijah and the other prophets of God. She encouraged the pouting Ahab to take Naboth's vineyard by having him murdered. Jezebel wasn't above idolatry, deceit, murder or vanity.

After her husband had been killed in battle, Jezebel knew her days were numbered. The new king Jehu was coming to visit her, and she connived to use her womanly wiles on him. "Then Jehu went to Jezreel. When Jezebel heard about it, she painted her eyes, arranged her hair and looked out of a window. As Jehu entered the gate, she asked, 'Have you come in peace, Zimri, you murderer of your master?'" (2 Kings 9:30-31).

Jehu didn't waste any time on her but commanded the nearby eunuchs to throw Jezebel out of the window. Her blood spattered the wall and the horses as they trampled her underfoot. Afterward, just as Elijah had prophesied, dogs devoured all of her body except her skull, feet and hands. What a bloody end to an evil, vain woman!

Perhaps Jezebel thought her looks could sway Jehu from his godly purpose. Maybe she thought she had to look good, no matter what. But her priorities were misguided and wrong. When she should have been begging for mercy, she was painting her eyes. Where do we set our priorities? How much do we spend on vanity?

It's Only Money?

Today, it's easy to spend money on ourselves. Often, beauty does not come cheap. When we stroll down any department store aisle, we see exorbitant prices on everything from clothes to makeup to exercise machines. Higher prices are seemingly justified by that constant reminder that "you get what you pay for." With that reasoning, expensive should always mean better. It doesn't. Brand-name products are often overpriced. Sometimes the only difference between brands is the designer label or name on the package. Clever advertising and packaging often make us believe we are getting more than we really are. Familiar products are frequently promoted as "new and improved." Cosmetic companies are masters of marketing. They use exotic technology to sound scientific and assert that their products will restore, repair, or create a more beautiful you. Many manufacturers create higher priced product lines with elegant packaging – boosting the price for the "exclusive formulas." But researchers have shown that these luxury products are not always better.[2]

With so many choices and price ranges, it is difficult to make our way through the maze of products on the market. We need to pray for wisdom and seek the advice of reliable sources to know if a product or service is really worth the price.

Suffering for Vanity

A French proverb states: "One must suffer to be beautiful."[3] Through the ages women have submitted to physical discomfort and outright pain in an attempt to become more attractive. Consider some beauty rites of the past that seem barbaric as well as bizarre.

Some cultures have valued the alteration and elimination of body parts. From ancient times until the 20th century, a Chinese female would have her feet bound so that they would remain small and she would not be called a "large-footed demon."[4] This practice, supposedly making her more helpless and eligible for marriage, caused her toes to bend, break and sometimes drop off!

Several Native American tribes and the Mayan Indians of Central America considered flattened heads beautiful and unworthy of hard labor. For this purpose they flattened a baby's skull by binding its head with boards.[5] Some African tribes prized large platter lips, stretched necks and earlobes, and body scarification for beauty.[6]

Dangerous chemicals were used by some women to improve their appearance. Medieval women applied a substance called "soliman," which contained mercury, to their faces to get rid of warts and spots. Unfortunately, it also got rid of the outer layer of skin and caused gum recession. It is amazing that more women did not die from lead-poisoning from the practice of whitening their faces with ceruse, a mixture of lead and vinegar.[7]

In the early 1900s, a Viennese doctor injected paraffin wax into his patients' faces to remove wrinkles – but it resulted in also having to remove whole sections of facial tissue infiltrated with solidified paraffin.[8]

Body shaping is not new. To achieve the sought-after hourglass figure, Victorian women had one or more ribs removed surgically.[9] In the 1920s the "nose shaper" was "a vicious-looking metal object, held over the nose by straps buckled round the head, and fitted with an array of screws which could be tightened to apply pressure to the offending width, length, bump or crookedness."[10]

Other cruelties of fashion include tight girdles (the first ones were worn by the Cretes around 1500 B.C.[11]), straitlaced corsets and uncomfortable shoes. The publication *Handbook of the Toilet* (1841) stated, "There hardly exists an Englishwoman whose toes are not folded over one another, each of those crooked and the nails destroyed, such were women's sufferings for vanity."[12]

Vanity Today

We are shocked at abuses of the past, but present-day vanity can be just as harmful. The alarming growth of eating disorders is one example. Anorexia nervosa is a disorder that usually affects teenage girls. Although they have access to all the food they need, they refuse to eat enough to remain healthy. This self-starvation is a reaction to the perceived societal mandate that one must be thin to be beautiful. If continued, this condition can lead to loss of menstrual periods, low heart rate, episodes of bulimia (binge eating), self-induced vomiting and even death.[13]

Many people have turned to cosmetic surgery to turn back the clock for a more youthful appearance. According to the American Academy of Cosmetic Surgery, cosmetic procedures topped 3.3 million in 1996. Most are performed on people aged 35 to 50. The most popular procedures were chemical peel, vein treatment, liposuction, laser resurfacing and eyelid surgery.[14] Other procedures include rhinoplasty, facelifts, demabrasion, breast enlargement and tummy tucks. Since most cosmetic fees are not covered by insurance, patients usually pay in advance out of their own pockets. Although doctors can use computer imaging to show a patient the possible results, there is no satisfaction guarantee of the outcome of these procedures. Some doctors lack the required expertise, and the horror stories of their scarred patients prove it. These real surgeries require recovery times of a few hours up to two years. Some surgeries must be repeated to retain the desired look. As with all operations there are risks, including infection, scarring, heart irregularities, blindness and, in some cases, death.[15]

How far should we go with cosmetic surgery? We read of Jesus healing people with physical deformities, and we are thankful for medical advances today that make possible the healing of disorders from birth defects, illness or injuries. But when it comes to "correcting" the natural effects of aging or simply trying to reach someone's standard of beauty, we must make wise decisions.

Such questions as these might help us arrive at a wise decision:

1. Is the blemish I want to have corrected so distracting that it hinders people from being able to relate to me?

2. Is my desire for cosmetic surgery only a sign that I am in denial of the fact of aging?

3. Do my signs of aging keep me from reaching a worthwhile goal, or is my desire to "correct" them only a sign of vanity?

4. Is my desire for cosmetic surgery an indication of low self-esteem that really needs to be corrected by healthier attitudes and self-acceptance?

Too High a Cost?

In all these examples, we see the extent to which some people go to be beautiful. Every Christian woman must consider her situation and ask herself: Is this worth the physical risks? Am I paying too high a price in my time or energy? Is this the best use of my financial resources? Should my expenditures of time and effort be spent in more heavenly pursuits?

It is appropriate for a Christian woman to want to look her best – for herself, for her husband and for others. But we must avoid paying too much for beauty in money, health or time. We should seek ways to maximize our efforts without minimizing what is really important. Consumer magazines can help us evaluate if a special-formula cosmetic is any better than the lower-priced brand. We can be wise shoppers. We can combine certain home beauty activities with other household tasks. We can remember that no definition of beauty should cause us to harm our bodies. We can refuse to be deceived by all the world's hype.

We're Worth It

A hair color company tells us their product costs a little more, but we're "worth it." We're worth it, all right, but not because we pay a higher price for products or procedures. One soul – your soul or mine – is worth more than the whole world (Matthew 16:26). We have already been "bought at a price" with the blood of Christ who died on the cross for our sins (1 Corinthians 7:23). Peter writes:

> For you know that it was not with perishable things such as silver or gold that you were redeemed from the empty way of life handed down to you from your forefathers, but with the precious blood of Christ, a lamb without blemish or defect. … Through him you believe in God, who raised him from the dead and glorified him, and so your faith and hope are in God (1 Peter 1:18-19, 21).

As Christian women, our faith is not in a knife to sculpt a prettier face or in a severe diet for a slimmer figure. Our hope is not in a jar. We are worthy because God makes us worthy, not because of how we look or what we can afford. First, we were created in the image of God. Then, at the highest cost imaginable, Jesus paid the price and made salvation possible for us. He resoundingly demonstrated that His children are worth it!

Inside Out

1. How does Jesus' answer to the Pharisees in Luke 16:13-15 apply to overspending on vanity today?

2. How do attractive advertising and packaging make us think we are getting more for our money than we really are?

3. Give some examples of the extremes to which women have gone to be beautiful.

4. Why do you think some women have suffered for vanity throughout history?

5. Why was body cutting forbidden, and what were the circumstances of this practice in these scriptures: Deuteronomy 14:1; 1 Kings 18:28; Jeremiah 41:4; 47:5?

6. Why were tattoos forbidden in the Old Testament (Leviticus 19:28)?

7. How should Jesus' teaching in Matthew 6:33 affect our beauty procedures and purchases?

8. What are some ways we can set the right priorities and become wiser in our shopping?

9. What did Jesus tell His followers to be on guard against in Luke 12:15?

10. What price did Christ pay for the church (Acts 20:28)?

The Way It Was

PAINTING UP AND FIXING UP

Although women today enjoy an array of cosmetic products, women of the past found ways to paint and fix up too. Many women used cosmetics extensively. Archaeologists have found curling irons, tweezers, ear spoons, ivory combs, bone hairpins, bodkins, alabaster ointment boxes, bronze razor blades four to six inches long, and little stone mills for grinding eye paint.[16] Women utilized cosmetic containers with metal and ivory kohl sticks and spoons, some elaborately carved and decorated.[17]

Egyptian, Greek and Roman women used compounds to become more attractive. Henna juice, which left an orange stain, was used to paint nails, feet, lips and hair. Women painted their eyebrows and eyelashes with galena, a bluish-gray mineral containing lead sulfide, and powdered lapis lazuli. To color their lips, they used cochineal, a concoction from dried insects.[18] They applied heavy black eyeliner to their eyes to make them look larger (2 Kings 9:30; Ezekiel 23:40). The name of Job's beautiful third daughter, Keren-Happuch, meant source of beauty or literally, "horn of eye paint" (Job 42:14).[19]

Men, as well as women, put on makeup and rouge. Their makeup consisted of chalk, milk, vermilion, oxide of lead, and black and blue paints.[20] One recipe for makeup included barley meal, ground pulse, eggs, ground antlers, narcissus bulbs, gum, honey and wheatflour from Tuscany. Another recipe called for Illyrian iris, grilled pale lupines, white lead, cooked beans and froth of red niter.[21] And we think our makeup is made from natural ingredients!

$\mathcal{E}$VE'S FIG LEAVES AND BEYOND

"The first costume on record was a hand-me-down – from the fig tree."

Evan Esar[1]

$\mathcal{I}$N THE GARDEN of Eden, Eve didn't have to worry about wearing clothes. Naked and unashamed, she didn't have to look in her closet and ponder what style or color she would wear. She had no concerns about hem lengths, missing buttons or ring around the collar. She was the first woman who honestly could say, "I don't have a thing to wear!"

But idyllic existence abruptly changed when Adam and Eve sinned against God. Ironically, as man and woman felt the need to hide from God spiritually, they also felt the need to hide physically. They made their first garments from fig leaves to hide their nakedness.

Ever since Adam and Eve discovered the naked truth of their disobedience and took cover in the fig leaves, mankind has been destined to wear clothes. Every age has had its form of immodest dress; ours is no different. In this modern world of indecent exposure, we as Christians have a special responsibility to wear clothes that are modest and appropriate for the occasion. Paul urges, "I also want women to dress modestly, with decency and propriety, not with braided hair or gold or pearls or expensive clothes, but with good deeds, appropriate for women who profess to worship God" (1 Timothy 2:9-10). Just as women wear clothes appropriate for their work, our clothes should match our profession of being God's children. Some usually modest women are not careful enough about their revealing necklines or see-through dresses. We should check the mirror to avoid the "toos" – too short, too tight, too sheer, too low or too clingy.[2] Styles can be both fashionable and modest; we just need to have the patience to find them. Edith Head, the famous Hollywood costumer, said, "Your dresses should be tight enough to show you're a woman and loose enough to show you're a lady."[3]

The saying that "clothes make the man" – or woman – shows the importance clothes can play in our lives. How important should clothes be to us as Christians? What insights about clothes can we gain from the Word of God?

The Meaning of Changing Clothes

We think nothing of changing our clothes, but in Bible times it meant more. Bathing was infrequent. Clothes were often expensive and hard to obtain, and many people had only one change of garments. A change of clothes could symbolize a change in attitude. In preparation for his move to Bethel, Jacob told his household to change their clothes and destroy the idols in their house (Genesis 35:2). After David's infant son died, David's attitude of supplication turned to acceptance as he washed, put on lotions and changed clothes (2 Samuel 12:20).

When the prophet Elijah prophesied doom for Ahab's family, the king tore his clothes and put on sackcloth (1 Kings 21:27). When Hezekiah was faced with the possible destruction of Jerusalem, he too tore his clothes and put on sackcloth (2 Kings 19:1). It was prophesied that when the princes of Tyre fell, they would mourn by taking off their embroidered robes (Ezekiel 26:16). Jonah's powerful preaching of God's judgment caused the heathen Ninevites to put on sackcloth in repentance (Jonah 3:5).

Changing clothes could also mean a change in a person's station in life. Tamar, dressing as a prostitute, went to extreme measures to obtain an heir and husband; then she put on her widow's clothes again (Genesis 38:14-15, 19). Captive King Jehoiachin put aside his prison clothes when the king of Babylon showed him favor for the rest of his life (2 Kings 25:27-30). Jesus graphically demonstrated His humble servant-like status when He put on a towel and washed His disciples' feet (John 13:4, 12).

The Age-Old Status Symbol

Since early civilizations, clothes have been used as a status symbol and often a basis for discrimination. Joseph's richly ornamented robe was a statement of his father, Jacob's, preference for him over his brothers. That robe ironically became a symbol of their hatred as they stripped it off Joseph, dipped it in goat's blood, and showed it to their father as proof of Joseph's death. Then when Joseph rose to second in command in Egypt, Pharaoh adorned him in the fine linen robes of Egypt to show his elevated position (Genesis 37:3-4, 31-33; 41:42). When Aaron and his sons were ordained to be priests, they were set apart for their prestigious office in priestly garments (Exodus 28:41). When the prodigal son returned home, his father demonstrated his favor by putting a ring on him and dressing him in the finest robe (Luke 15:22).

In ancient times, even the color of a garment denoted status. Purple was a prized color because the dye was so costly to make. The dye was extracted from the murex shellfish, a snail found in the Mediterranean. Solomon asked skilled men from Tyre to help make the purple fabric for the temple (2 Chronicles 2:7). In His story of the rich man and Lazarus, Jesus made a point to mention the fine linen and purple that arrayed the rich man (Luke 16:19). Though done in mockery, Jesus' purple robe represented the honor and authority due a king (Mark 15:17). Lydia, an early Philippian Christian businesswoman, undoubtedly sold purple material to a rich clientele (Acts 16:14).[4]

People use clothes as a status symbol today as well. Because certain brand names are more expensive, wearing them can make one feel a notch above. Some brand names are so important to some people that they are willing to steal and even kill for them. Brand-name clothes usually cost more, and they can also be of higher quality. That isn't always the case, however. So we need to ask ourselves,

"Why am I buying a certain brand? Is it worth the cost? Is the quality or fit better, or is it only for the label? Do I think this brand makes me more worthwhile?" Special brands of clothing do not determine our worth. If we are Christians, we already wear the greatest name by the best Designer!

James warns of the danger of using clothes to discriminate against another by contrasting a man wearing a gold ring and fine clothes with a poor man in shabby clothes in worship. He wrote, "If you show special attention to the man wearing fine clothes and say, 'Here's a good seat for you,' but say to the poor man, 'You stand there,' or, 'Sit on the floor by my feet,' have you not discriminated among yourselves and become judges with evil thoughts?" (James 2:3-4). Likewise, we need to be careful not to show favoritism to someone who is well-dressed and who sports a designer label over the one who is mismatched and poorly dressed.

Stretching Our Wardrobe

Today we are blessed with an endless variety of clothing choices. That's what fashion is all about – more choices and changes so we will think we need to buy more. Does that mean that our closets should be bulging? Ideally not. Let's look at some practical guidelines for shopping wisely and stretching our wardrobes without enlarging our closets:

1. Discover what looks good on you. Study why you like certain colors and which ones bring out the best in you. What styles and textures flatter your figure?

2. Get a quick preview of new styles by glancing through major store fashion and sewing catalogs. These come out several months before the season. Determine how you can use what you have or buy accessories like jewelry and scarves for a new look.

3. When you need an article of clothing, determine if it is worth the cost. Figure the cost-per-wearing by dividing the purchase price by the anticipated number of wearings. A blouse costing $30 worn 10 times a year ($30 ÷ 10 = $3 cost-per-wearing) would be cheaper than a blouse costing $5 worn only once ($5 ÷ 1 = $5 cost-per-wearing).[5]

4. Rotate what you wear. Most women never wear 90 percent of what is in their closets.[6] When something is worn, you could move it from the front to the back of your closet.

5. Buy clothes that go with at least one item you already have, but preferably more. Coordinate your clothes by color by taking along color swatches (snippets of seams or hems) when you shop.

6. Educate yourself to know good quality construction details in clothes like matching plaids, even hems and symmetric lapels. A high price tag does not guarantee that a garment is made well.[7]

7. Learn to sew. Get a friend to teach you, or take a course at a sewing center or school. Even if you only learn to repair garments, your knowledge will save you money.

8. Expand your shopping horizons. Check out outlets, off-price stores and consignment shops for bargains. Don't forget catalogs.

9. Timing is worth a lot. Don't wait until the night before you need a special outfit to go shopping, or you might have to settle for pricey duds. Avoid crowded shopping times. Shop after-season sales for next year.[8]

10. Pray for wisdom in your shopping. Practice self-control to pass up clothes that aren't "you," even though they are on sale or have a designer label.

Clothe Yourself with Contentment

Paul wrote in 1 Timothy 6:6-8, "But godliness with contentment is great gain. For we brought nothing into the world, and we can take nothing out of it. But if we have food and clothing, we will be content with that." Jesus said:

> And why do you worry about clothes? See how the lilies of the fields grow. They do not labor or spin. Yet I tell you that not even Solomon in all his splendor was dressed like one of these. If that is how God clothes the grass of the field, which is here today and tomorrow is thrown into the fire, will he not much more clothe you, O you of little faith? (Matthew 6:28-30).

How can we allow our closets to overflow with clothes we can't or don't wear when other people are in need of clothing? How can we waste money on extravagant purchases? John addresses this in 1 John 3:17-18: "If anyone has material possessions and sees his brother in need but has no pity on him, how can the love of God be in him? Dear children, let us not love with words or tongue but with actions and in truth." John says our love for people is demonstrated in action. That can sometimes translate into cleaning out our closets and making wiser purchases!

Jesus warns us of closet stuffing in Matthew 6:19-21:

> Do not store up for yourselves treasures on earth, where moth and rust destroy, and where thieves break in and steal. But store up for yourselves treasures in heaven, where moth and rust do not destroy, and where thieves do not break in and steal. For where your treasure is, there your heart will be also.

We might try a loose paraphrase in today's language: "Don't cram your closets full of stuff that can get moth-eaten, rusty or stolen. Anyway, it will eventually go out of style! Instead, put your confidence, time and money into things that last – spiritual things. Nothing can harm those – and they never will go out of style."[9]

Inside Out

1. How can a woman be sure her clothing is modest?

2. What could changing clothes mean to the people in Scripture?

3. In Bible times how could clothing be used as a status symbol? How is clothing used that way today?

4. What are some ways we can stretch our wardrobe?

5. What part did clothes play in the trouble these people had?
   a. Jacob (Genesis 27:15, 27)
   b. Achan (Joshua 7:21)
   c. Samson (Judges 14:12)
   d. Gehazi (2 Kings 5:23)

6. Why did Jesus tell the 12 disciples not to take an extra tunic or sandals on their journey to preach (Matthew 10:10)?

7. What was unusual about the remaining garment of Jesus that the soldiers cast lots for at the cross (John 19:23-24)?

8. How should we clothe ourselves spiritually?
    Isaiah 51:9
    Romans 13:14
    Galatians 3:27
    Colossians 3:12
    1 Peter 5:5

9. What are some things we should take off and put on?
    Take off
    a. Romans 13:12
    b. Ephesians 4:22
    c. Ephesians 4:25
    d. Colossians 3:9
    Put on
    Romans 13:12
    Ephesians 4:24
    Ephesians 6:11, 13
    Colossians 3:10, 14

10. What is described as being washed, stain-free and wrinkle-free (Ephesians 5:26-27)?

SHOWING THEIR COLORS

Because styles for women in Bible times changed little, it was color that gave women's clothes their distinction. Surprisingly, many colors could be worn. Deborah tells of Sisera's mother longing for her son's return so she could indulge herself with his spoils: "colorful garments as plunder for Sisera, colorful garments embroidered, highly embroidered garments for my neck – all this as plunder?" (Judges 5:30).

Many colors were made from plant and mineral dyes. Saffron and pomegranates yielded yellow. From safflower and madder root came a fiery red, and from woad, an herb, came a heavenly blue.[10] Other colors included amethyst, sea-green, Paphian myrtle, acorn, pale rose, Thracian crane and almond.

Purple, the epitome of extravagance in color, actually covered a wide range from blue to red to purple. Among these were hard and brilliant scarlet, dark rose and amethyst.[11] This might explain why the color of Jesus' robe of mockery is called scarlet (Matthew 27:28) and also purple (Mark 15:17; John 19:2). David mentioned one of these colors in his lament over Saul's death: "O daughters of Israel, weep for Saul, who clothed you in scarlet and finery, who adorned your garments with ornaments of gold" (2 Samuel 1:24). The virtuous woman clothed her family in scarlet and herself in purple (Proverbs 31:21-22). These were principally murex dyes that Tyre and later Palestine made into a profitable industry.[12]

The final word in color fashion must have been that of the princess in Psalm 45:13 – a gown interwoven with gold!

Chapter 10

FIT FOR THE KING

"The road to flab
is paved with
good intentions."

Elaine St. James[1]

WHAT IF YOU could find something that would make you look and feel better with a minimum of expense? This something could give you a sense of accomplishment and well-being and help beat depression. It would make your body more efficient at burning fat. It could help your lungs and heart work more efficiently, as well as help keep you more productive and youthful.[2]

Sounds good. Is this a new miracle drug or secret formula? No, it's only exercise! With so many benefits, it's difficult to see why Americans aren't all involved in some kind of regular physical activity. Christians should make every effort to keep healthy and fit:

> Don't you know that you yourselves are God's temple and that God's Spirit lives in you? If anyone destroys God's temple, God will destroy him; for God's temple is sacred, and you are that temple (1 Corinthians 3:16-17).

Unfortunately, God's sacred temple is being destroyed by lack of use. Forty percent of Americans don't exercise at all, and another

40 percent exercise sporadically. For many, the fitness frenzy of a few years ago has fizzled![3]

Wimps for God?

We do not read of biblical women working out to their favorite exercise video. Instead, they were working out in the pasture, the grain field and the vineyard. They did not have the time or the need for recreational exercise because their lives demanded an active body just for their very existence. They didn't have to worry about getting enough exercise during the day. Their lifestyles probably made them exhausted by nightfall.

In their basically agrarian society, most women in Scripture were housewives with all the duties that role entailed – cooking, baking, churning, spinning, weaving, grinding grain and drawing water for the household as well as for guests and livestock (Proverbs 31:13-27). For her many responsibilities, the virtuous woman in Proverbs also seemed to be physically fit: "She sets about her work vigorously; her arms are strong for her tasks" (v. 17). Women at this time had to have a fairly good sense of balance because they carried heavy loads on their heads – pitchers of water, dried flat cakes of straw, and dung for fuel.[4] Some women gleaned from the fields (Ruth 2:3) and tended sheep (Genesis 29:9; Exodus 2:16). Others were involved in the sale of real estate (Proverbs 31:16; Acts 5:1), fabric (16:14) and tents (18:2-3).[5] Barak called Deborah, the prophetess, to gather a nation for battle (Judges 4:8-9).

In contrast, our lives are full of time- and labor-saving appliances. Even active people don't feel the need to exercise because they are always busy doing things, but they could be far from healthy. Taking care of their bodies is the last item on their hectic to-do lists. They might work at a full-time job sitting at a desk and attend evening meetings where they sit some more. They mow the grass on a riding lawn mower, play games sitting at a table, and run a lot of errands in a car.[6] Will Rogers wrote, "The trouble with us is, America is just muscle-bound from holding a steering wheel. The only place we are calloused from work is the bottom of our driving toe."[7]

Too old, too fat, too out of shape, too little time, too many responsibilities, no place to exercise – the excuses go on and on. But why do we really neglect to exercise our bodies? Author Stormie Omartian suggests some reasons why we struggle to keep fit:

Ignorance: "I just don't understand the reasons for doing this, so I'm just going to forget it."

Fear of failure: "I've failed so many times, and I don't want to fail again."

Losing touch with reality: "I think I can beat the odds and be healthy without exercising."

Willful neglect: "I do not want to exercise, and I'm not going to!"

Lack of vision or motivation: "I know what I should do, but I'm a loser anyway. Who cares if I'm thin, fat, sick or healthy?"

Having unrealistic expectations: "I'll never have shapely legs or a flat stomach – why should I try?"[8]

Whatever our shape or size, we should find a way to exercise. Why? To maintain our health so we can be effective in serving God. Jesus, our example, grew in four basic ways – mentally, spiritually, socially and physically (Luke 2:52). These varied facets of His life represented a well-rounded person, and they offer an excellent model for us to follow. We should try to achieve the balance that Jesus had in His life.

Good News

The good news is that there are more ways to exercise than side-straddle hops and toe touches! In fact, it's best to do a combination of activities so that we utilize different muscles and don't get bored with the same old thing. Aerobic activities are great for improving our health, but no matter how fit we are, we also need to stretch daily and to strengthen our muscles every other day. Here are some possibilities:

• Aerobics (low and high impact)
• Racquet sports (racquetball, tennis, squash, badminton)
• Martial arts
• Exercise machines (weights, rowing, treadmills)

- Gymnastics
- Skiing (downhill, water, cross-country)
- Biking (stationary, cross-country)
- Floor exercises (audio and video tapes, exercise classes)
- Swimming (laps, aquarobics)
- Team sports (volleyball, soccer, basketball, softball)
- Horseback riding
- Skating (ice, in-line, roller)
- Running (long-distance, sprinting, jogging) [9]
- Walking (the exercise Jesus did)

Several scriptures refer to Jesus walking, healing and teaching as He went. Because Jesus didn't have a home (Luke 9:58), He probably didn't own a horse or donkey; remember how He had to borrow the donkey when He entered Jerusalem (Mark 11:1-11; Luke 19:28-34)? The walking helped to keep Him fit physically.

Several kinds of walking exist: hiking, strolling, race walking and wogging – a combination of jogging and walking. Walking is cheap, pleasurable, easy, convenient and almost injury free. This form of exercise is as close as your front door or your treadmill. It's something almost everyone can do.

Taking the Plunge

How do we get started? Before you start jogging six miles a day, it is very important to consult a doctor and determine your physical condition and any health problems that might affect your progress. Take a health history of yourself and your family to learn if it includes heart disease or other factors that might bear on your decision to exercise. You might be surprised at what you discover.[10]

Start small; build up to greater activity. Little changes in our lifestyles can make a positive difference. Climb the stairs instead of taking the elevator, or park farther away to walk more. Find a buddy to exercise with you, or involve your family and make each other accountable. If we wait for a convenient day to exercise, that day will probably never come.[11]

Avoid the "terrible toos" – too much, too hard, too soon, with too little preparation. Besides getting sore muscles and torn ligaments, you can become discouraged and quit soon after you get started. The overdo syndrome has beaten many a weekend warrior![12] Some women get so caught up in exercising that they become "fitaholics." They become compulsive about working out longer and pushing harder until they harm their bodies. They set unrealistic goals and endure disrupted menstrual cycles, stress and strained muscles all in the name of being fit. They will not rest after an injury. "Working out" sometimes takes the place of working out problems. Called the "twin obsessions," compulsive exercising and chronic dieting often work together in women who are trying to lose weight but go too far.

Instead of burning out, assess your condition, set realistic goals and start slowly. Buy good-quality shoes, but don't feel compelled to invest in expensive machinery to work out efficiently. Stretch yourself a little farther each time, but don't continue if it hurts. The no-gain-without-pain is a myth. Instead of focusing on competition or weight loss, concentrate on the three Fs of movement – fulfillment, fitness and fun.[13]

The advantages of exercise far outweigh the time and planning it might take to rearrange our lives to make it possible. Research has found that at least 20 to 30 minutes of aerobic activity three to five times a week can help maintain a healthy lifestyle. Isn't this a comparatively small investment to make for a healthier and perhaps even longer life?

God Deserves Our Best

If we are to be effective Christians, we need to be physically fit for God's work. A healthy, vibrant person will have more energy to work in the Lord's kingdom. This does not mean that disabled or sick people cannot be effective for God. Sometimes these conditions are beyond our control, and God can use every situation and every person for good. But we should try to be as healthy and fit as our circumstances allow because the Lord deserves our best.

God made our physical bodies to glorify Him, for He needs "everyone who is called by my name, whom I created for my glory, whom I formed and made" (Isaiah 43:7). Paul echoes, "For we are God's workmanship, created in Christ Jesus to do good works, which God prepared in advance for us to do" (Ephesians 2:10).

Wouldn't it seem that we would want to maintain this marvelous machine of a body that God created just for His purpose?

The Greeks and Romans emphasized bodily development in Paul's day. Paul used metaphors for Christianity such as running a race. He knew, however, that the most important exercise was spiritual. He wrote Timothy to "train yourself to be godly. For physical training is of some value, but godliness has value for all things, holding promise for both the present life and the life to come" (1 Timothy 4:7-8). Later Paul stated that each one of us can be "an instrument for noble purposes, made holy, useful to the Master and prepared to do any good work" (2 Timothy 2:21). If we are to be holy, useful and prepared for the Lord's work, we need to be as fit as we can be – spiritually and physically. When we became Christians, we were born into a royal family. Our goal is not just to be fit, but fit for the King.

Inside Out

1. What are some reasons for exercising?

2. What are some excuses for not exercising?

3. What are some activities of women in Bible times that helped keep them fit?

4. What are some activities that can keep us fit?

5. What are some characteristics of "fitaholics"?

6. How can we use moderation in our activities and fitness purchases?

7. What is the main purpose of our bodies?

8. With all his tribulations listed in 2 Corinthians 11:23-28, why was it important for Paul to be as fit as he could?

9. What reference to physical sports does Paul allude to in these scriptures, and how do they apply to the Christian life?
   1 Corinthians 9:24-27   Philippians 3:13-14
   Galatians 5:7   2 Timothy 4:6-8

10. What does God's Word say will bring "health to your body and nourishment to your bones" (Proverbs 3:7-8)?

The Way It Was

THE ANCIENT SWEET TOOTH

We aren't the only ones who hanker for something sweet. Ancient people had a sweet tooth, too! The principal bakers of fancy cakes and candy were women (1 Samuel 8:13). They sold their products in the marketplaces of their towns. Ingredients such as honey, nuts, dates and gum arabic were mixed and cooked to produce sweets of a definite color, texture and flavor. Then they were shaped by spinning or rolling them into strips that could be cut.[14]

The very rich and royalty could afford to have their dainties prepared by experts (Genesis 49:20). But the common man had to enjoy sweets whenever he could find them. He was more likely to eat honey from wild bees. Samson found honey in the lion's carcass (Judges 14:8-9). Moses spoke of finding it among the rocks (Deuteronomy 32:13).

The honey in some Bible references probably refers to the thick syrup of boiled-down grape juice called "dibs." Although honey from wild bees was sometimes available, bee hives were not kept until Roman times. Dibs was spread on bread like our jelly and sometimes diluted with water to make a sweet drink.[15]

Other syrupy drinks were flavored with scented waters from the blooms of roses, violets and orange trees. These drinks were kept in large, tightly sealed bottles for a cool, refreshing drink in the summer.[16] And we thought *our* flavored spring waters were original!

Chapter 11

ℱOOD, GLORIOUS FOOD

"When it comes to eating, you can sometimes help yourself more by helping yourself less."
Richard Armour[1]

ℱOOD CAN HAVE A powerful grip on us whether we are over, under or around our acceptable weight. We find it easy to daydream about our next meal at the all-you-can-eat buffet. We marvel at all the varieties of edibles at the grocery store and clamor to try them regardless of price or healthfulness. TV commercials and magazine covers boast appetizing layouts of everything from fondue to stew, juice to mousse, and cakes to shakes.

Food has more meaning than something to sustain life – warm memories of the fellowship of family and friends, comfort, a reward, guilt, addiction. These feelings can run deep and have real consequences for our lives, but would Jesus act like we sometimes do about food? What attitude should we have about this God-given gift?

A God-Given Gift

In the Garden of Eden, God provided a vast array of food for Adam and Eve. They could choose anything they might desire except the fruit from the Tree of the Knowledge of Good and Evil. Eve and Adam succumbed to the devil's temptation to eat of that very forbidden fruit. As a result, sin entered the world.

After the flood, God told Noah, "Everything that lives and moves will be food for you" (Genesis 9:3). The only stipulation was that no meat with the lifeblood still in it should be eaten (v. 4). Later, the Law of Moses brought other stipulations. Rules were given regarding clean and unclean foods (Leviticus 11). Other laws governed how food was to be used in sacrifice (17:1-12; 19:5-8; 22).

These food laws became very important to the Jews and distinguished them from other nations. Daniel, captured by the Babylonians, courageously abstained from King Nebuchadnezzar's food, perhaps because it was defiled by idol worship or out of loyalty to Jewish dietary restrictions (Daniel 1:8-16).

In time, various food rituals evolved, and the Jewish leaders tried to make these traditions binding. Because of their preoccupation with food rules and regulations, the Jewish leaders confronted Jesus several times during His ministry. He was criticized for eating with sinners and tax collectors (Luke 5:30). The Pharisees and teachers, who ceremoniously washed their hands and dishes, were appalled when Jesus' disciples ate with ceremonially unclean hands. Jesus told them, "You have let go of the commands of God and are holding on to the traditions of men" (Mark 7:8). He told them that unclean food does not make a person unclean, but a dirty heart filled with sin. Another time, Jesus asked His critics and followers, "Is not life more important than food?" (Matthew 6:25).

Fast or Feast?

Fasting, the abstinence from food or drink, had been a long-held Jewish tradition by the time of Jesus. It often accompanied sorrowful prayer, tearing the clothes and wearing sackcloth and ashes. The element of sorrow was so strong that the Jews were forbidden to fast on the Sabbath, a day of gladness. The exception was the Day of Atonement or Yom Kippur. This fast, mentioned in Acts 27:9, was the only absolute fast, no food or drink, required under Jewish law; noncompliance meant death (Leviticus 23:26-32). Only pregnant and nursing mothers and children were exempt. The day was spent in meditation, prayer and public worship.[2]

The Bible contains many examples of fasting for several different purposes. A Jew saw death as an uncertain adventure, so it was an occasion for deep mourning and therefore fasting.[3] Fasting also demonstrated penitence for sins. Supplication for God's help was another reason for fasting.[4] The most important example of fasting as supplication to God is the 40-day fast of Jesus in preparation for His ministry. At Jesus' hungriest moment, the devil tempted Him to turn stones into bread. Jesus withstood the test by quoting Scripture: "Man does not live on bread alone, but on every word that comes from the mouth of God" (Matthew 4:4).

With fasting important to the Jews, it is no surprise that the Pharisees wondered why Jesus' disciples did not follow this custom as John's followers did (9:14-17; Mark 2:18-22; Luke 5:33-39). Jesus answered that His disciples didn't need to fast when He, the Bridegroom, was with them; it was the custom for weddings to be happy. After He was gone, they would feel the need to fast again, but not in the same way as the legalism of the past.

After Jesus' ascension to heaven, fasting was most often associated with supplication rather than mourning and penitence. In setting apart Paul and Barnabas for mission work, the Antioch church fasted and prayed (Acts 13:2-3). In appointing elders in Lystra, Iconium and Antioch, Paul and Barnabas prayed and fasted (14:23).[5] Paul, however, never commanded fasting in his letters. Early Christianity was characterized primarily not by fasting but by breaking bread, prayer and fellowship (2:42).

Today, a Christian may fast with the right motives. Scriptural fasting is not a public show or an insincere or artificial ritual (Matthew 6:16-18; Luke 18:12). Fasting should not take the place of prayer, penitence or good works. Neither should godly fasting be seen as political activism, such as in a hunger strike, or be done for unholy purposes (Acts 23:12). Rather, fasting is an act of devotion unique to each individual in purpose and circumstance that can draw a Christian closer to God and His will.

The Trouble with Food

The trouble with food is when we allow it to control us. We can be preoccupied with food in many ways, but here are two extremes.

Gluttony can be a problem for anyone of any weight; gluttony is simply eating too much. We get images of a glutton as a medieval lord throwing turkey drumsticks across his shoulder, but are we much different as we overload our plates at church fellowship meals? Gluttony is often paired with drunkenness: "Do not join those who drink too much wine or gorge themselves on meat, for drunkards and gluttons become poor, and drowsiness clothes them in rags" (Proverbs 23:20-21). When a person is drunk and drowsy from overeating, he will be in no shape to work. We are also told that gluttons can keep bad company – liars and evil brutes (Titus 1:12).

Paul discloses the real problem of gluttons in Philippians 3:19 – "their god is their stomach." Instead of putting God on the throne in his life, the glutton's stomach rules his life, and filling it is his goal. No wonder some people can't seem to quit eating; they are trying to fill the bottomless pit of a god.

If Jesus is made the Lord of our lives, He can teach us to say no to "ungodliness and worldly passions, and to live self-controlled, upright and godly lives in this present age" (Titus 2:12). Worldly passions can include a passion for chocolate or pizza or freshly baked sweet rolls if we allow that passion to dominate our lives. However, God can give us His willpower to overcome. "For God did not give us a spirit of timidity, but a spirit of power, of love and of self-discipline" (2 Timothy 1:7). Christians should be characterized by moderation and not excess.

An opposite extreme of gluttony is anorexia – eating too little. Some people in medieval times actually became anorexic to become what they considered to be more holy. Along with beating themselves, they took harsh measures to eat as little as possible to have more power over their bodies. They felt that "to obliterate every human feeling of pain, fatigue, sexual desire, and hunger is to be master of oneself."[7] This self denial was damaging and unnecessary to be a Christian. In Colossians 2:22-23 Paul criticized rigid, man-made rules like these:

> These are all destined to perish with use, because they are based
> on human commands and teachings. Such regulations indeed
> have an appearance of wisdom, with their self-imposed wor-

ship, their false humility and their harsh treatment of the body, but they lack any value in restraining sensual indulgence.

Restraint and control are taken to extremes with today's anorexic. In a world where she thinks she can control little else in her life, the anorexic can take pride in controlling her eating. She can do what other people cannot do – refuse to eat. She has a distorted body image and denies her need for food. Anorexia requires medical attention. This serious health problem has physical and spiritual implications.[8]

Eating More Wisely

Food doesn't have to control us. With God's help, we can forget about focusing on food and learn to eat more wisely. Here are some ways that can help:

1. Eat slowly. It takes about 20 minutes for your stomach to tell your brain when it is satisfied. When you are full, stop. Put down your fork, and sip your beverage between bites. Place your napkin over your plate so you won't eat more.[9]

2. Think smaller. Cut portions in bite-size pieces, and eat one at a time. Use smaller plates and divide helpings in half. The recommended portion of meat for a meal is only about the size of a deck of playing cards.

3. Enjoy your food and allow other people to enjoy theirs. Don't talk about calories, dieting or fat content. Savor each bite. Use attractive place settings.[10] Paul wrote that everything God created, including food, is good and should be received with thanksgiving (1 Timothy 4:3).

4. If you have a choice in menu preparation, offer a variety of foods. Concentrate your shopping on the healthier grocery store perimeter (vegetables, fruits, meat, dairy products). Strive for balance and moderation.

5. Don't focus on food so much. Think more about spiritual things (Philippians 4:8). Paul told the Corinthians that they should not be mastered by food or sex or other temporal desires but rather should devote their bodies to the Lord (1 Corinthians 6:12-13). Eat to live rather than live to eat.

Never Go Hungry Again

In feeding the multitudes, Jesus acknowledged the people's need for physical sustenance, but He chided them afterward because they followed Him only for physical food. He urged them, "Do not work for food that spoils, but for food that endures to eternal life, which the Son of Man will give you" (John 6:27). Jesus proclaimed, "I am the bread of life. He who comes to me will never go hungry, and he who believes in me will never be thirsty. … If a man eats of this bread, he will live forever" (vv. 35, 51).

Erwin Lutzer observed, "If you are not nourished by the Bread of heaven, you will stuff yourself with crumbs from the world. Real nourishment comes only from Jesus Christ. You'll be eternally sorry if you exchange real nourishment for crumbs."[11] Why settle for crumbs when a feast awaits us?

Inside Out

1. What were the laws governing foods that were clean and unclean and those used in sacrifices? (Leviticus 11, 17, 22)

2. Who fasted in these scriptures, and why? Who engaged in an absolute fast for 40 days? for three days?

Exodus 34:28	Judges 20:26
1 Samuel 14:24	1 Samuel 31:13
2 Samuel 1:12	2 Samuel 3:35
2 Samuel 12:16	1 Kings 21:27
1 Chronicles 10:12	2 Chronicles 20:3
Esther 4:3	Ezra 8:21-23
Ezra 10:6	Jonah 3:5
Acts 9:9	

3. What are some right and wrong motives for fasting?

4. Why do gluttony and anorexia have spiritual as well as physical implications?

5. What temptations in the Bible involved food?

6. How are we tempted by food today?

7. What are some ways we can overcome these temptations?

8. What foods were involved with these "firsts"?
    a. The first sin
    b. Noah's first job after leaving the ark
    c. Samson's first riddle
    d. Jesus' first miracle

9. What did Jesus mean when He spoke of eating His flesh and drinking His blood (John 6:50-57)?

10. What was Jesus' food that the disciples knew nothing about (John 4:32)?

A ROYAL SPREAD

*C*an you imagine someone so obese that when a foot-and-a-half long sword was plunged into his belly, the handle disappeared in his flesh (Judges 3:22)? So was the demise of the "very fat" Eglon, king of Moab (v. 17). Perhaps we more easily can see how a king could get that fat when we consider how royal tables were spread.

In Israel's most prosperous period, Solomon's daily provisions were 185 bushels of flour, 375 bushels of meal, 10 head of stall-fed cattle, 20 of pasture-fed cattle, 100 sheep and goats, deer, gazelles, roebucks and choice fowl (1 Kings 4:22-23). This doesn't mean that Solomon ate this much himself, but it certainly indicates the bounty available. When the queen of Sheba traveled to see Solomon's greatness, she was impressed by the food on his table (10:4-5).

An even better picture of how prosperity can turn royalty to pride, excess and gluttony is found in Esther. After 180 days of showing off the splendor of his kingdom, King Xerxes gave a seven-day banquet with wine served in different gold goblets and no limits on the amount. No wonder Xerxes was in high spirits from wine when he called for Vashti.

Kings weren't the only ones who gorged themselves. Amos had no sympathy for gluttonous women: "Hear this word, you cows of Bashan on Mount Samaria, you women who oppress the poor and crush the needy and say to your husbands, 'Bring us some drinks!' " (4:1). These overstuffed females reminded Amos of the cows who grazed the fertile grasslands of Bashan, the land east of the Sea of Galilee.[12]

Chapter 12

AGING WITH GRACE

"It's not how old you are but how you are old."

Marie Dressler[1]

FROM THE MOMENT of our birth we start growing old. Originally Adam and Eve were destined to live forever in the Garden of Eden. The result of their sin brought disease, aging and eventually death to us all.

Considering that growing older is inevitable, why is it so difficult for some of us to accept? We scoff at man's fruitless search for the elusive Fountain of Youth. Yet some of us battle wrinkles, gray hair and age spots with obsessive passion. Many of us spend countless hours and too much money trying to look and feel younger. As Phyllis Diller quipped, "I've worked so hard on staying young, it's beginning to age me!"[2]

As a society, more of us are living longer; yet the cultural norm is to try to look young as long as we can. We look at the well-preserved faces of film stars and marvel how they can look so young after all these years. Cary Grant admitted, "When people tell you how young you look, they are also telling you how old you are."[3]

How should we as Christian women approach the reality of aging? Should we fight it with all our resources, or is there a more godly way to confront aging?

Society's View of Aging

Several trends have an impact on aging in our society. America has been called a narcissistic society, where its citizens live to satisfy their own needs for individualism and self-gratification. Great emphasis is placed on the present, with little concern for the past or the future. We are obsessed with our physical looks, trying desperately to slow the effects of aging on the body. Ours is a youth culture – age is feared rather than respected.

Many people in our society today see getting older as a dreaded fate. Often senior citizens, once considered effective in their roles, are treated as obsolete and unwanted. Many have not adequately prepared for retirement and its implications and feel useless and patronized, unable to find their new place in life.

Changes in the nature of the family affect the aged as well. With fewer children born into families, more women working outside the home, and an increase in the number of divorces and broken homes, family members may not be able to care for older people who need help. With our busy lives and mobile society, is the sad fact that in some cases the elderly feel alienated from their children because of physical and emotional distance.[4]

All these rather depressing factors help us better understand why getting older is not always appreciated in our society. No wonder it seems important to appear younger. We need to recognize society's view of aging, but we don't have to embrace it. Let's check out some important truths about aging in the Bible.

The Bible's View of Aging

In God's plan, aging is considered inevitable, with birth and death as the bookends of life. In Ecclesiastes we read, "There is a time for everything, and a season for every activity under heaven; a time to be born and a time to die. ... He has made everything beautiful in its time" (Ecclesiastes 3:1-2, 11). After Adam and Eve's sin in the garden, people became mortal, living a certain number of days (Psalm 39:4; 90:10), then returning to the dust from which they came (Genesis 2:7; 3:19). Approaching death, David told Solomon, "I am about to go the way of all the earth" (1 Kings 2:2). Age and death were not considered a problem, just a part of life's journey.

In biblical times early death was viewed negatively because a person would not reach his full potential. When 39-year-old Hezekiah was destined to die, he asked, "In the prime of my life must I go through the gates of death and be robbed of the rest of my years?" (Isaiah 38:10).

Death in advanced age was considered a blessing from God. Thus, the elderly were considered especially blessed. "Gray hair is a crown of splendor; it is attained by a righteous life" (Proverbs 16:31). Such men as Abraham (Genesis 25:8), Isaac (35:28-29), Job (Job 42:16-17), David (1 Chronicles 29:28) and Jehoiada (2 Chronicles 24:15) died old and full of years. Proverbs 10:27 sums up this belief: "The fear of the Lord adds length to life, but the years of the wicked are cut short."[5]

So old age in the Bible was accepted, even welcomed, because it was seen as favor from God. But God's Word does not sugarcoat the realities of aging. The elderly Isaac's eyesight failed him (Genesis 27:1) as did his son Jacob's (48:10) and the priest Eli's (1 Samuel 4:15). Other scriptures note potential problems of old age such as obesity (v. 18), loss of sexual desire and lack of circulation (1 Kings 1:1-4), problems with the feet (15:23), and woman's inability to conceive (Genesis 18:13). Barzillai related his personal problems of aging to King David:

> I am now eighty years old. Can I tell the difference between what is good and what is not? Can your servant taste what he eats and drinks? Can I still hear the voices of men and women singers? Why should your servant be an added burden to my lord the king? (2 Samuel 19:35).[6]

Values of Aging

The Bible affirms important roles for the elderly. The aged had long been valued for their wisdom gained through years of living.

Job 12:12 expresses it well: "Is not wisdom found among the aged? Does not long life bring understanding?"

Although the old are not always wiser (Ecclesiastes 4:13), they often can be springs of knowledge and discernment. In the early days of Israel the elders would dispense judgment at the city gates (Numbers 11:16-17; Ruth 4:1-12). In the church, elders in New Testament times and now are called to make wise decisions and to lead the flock (1 Timothy 5:17; Titus 1:5-9). Older women are to teach the younger (2:3-5).[7]

Respect for the aged is shown in different ways in the Bible. People honored seniors by rising in their presence (Leviticus 19:32), supporting parents and in-laws (Ruth 2:11-12) and listening to their advice (Proverbs 1:8-9). Paul echoed this respect in his treatment of seniors: "Do not rebuke an older man harshly, but exhort him as if he were your father. Treat ... older women as mothers" (1 Timothy 5:1-2). The early church provided for widows who had no other support (vv. 3-10). The most touching example of caring for widows came from Jesus on the cross as He asked John to take care of His mother, Mary (John 19:26-27).[8]

Acceptance Is the Key

In all these scriptures, we don't see an obsessive concern for the inevitable changes in looks that aging brings. Fortunately, God is not impressed nor deceived by external appearances. Stephen Sapp writes:

In the sacrificial scheme of Old Testament religion, the object offered to God had to be unblemished, perfect, in its prime, in order to be worthy. The heart of Christian theology, on the other hand, is the affirmation that the only perfect sacrifice, the most pleasing and acceptable body ever offered to God, was the crucified body of Jesus of Nazareth – a beaten, humiliated body ... responsible for the restoration of the relationship between God and his creatures lost. ... For an older person today, then to feel that he or she is less worthy, less acceptable, because of the deterioration of the body runs contrary to the fundamental message of the Christian faith.

Christians, recognizing that the human being is more than just body, should accept and value a person no matter what condition the body is in.[9]

Acceptance – that is the key to aging with grace. The older woman can learn to accept herself and other people more easily. The physical characteristics that used to be such glaring faults can become her own distinctive trademarks. Time can temper her impatience and discontent with herself. She can choose role models who grow older along with her. She can accept more fully herself as God made her and give up unrealistic expectations for perfection.[10]

However, growing older is no excuse for getting frumpy, fat and faded. Acceptance of our aging self does not mean becoming apathetic to our appearance. Some women give up on themselves after reaching a certain age. God accepts us, but He wants us to be the best we can be. After all, we are His representatives to the world. We don't have to be obsessed with looking younger; instead, we can learn to appreciate whatever age we are and be content with what we cannot change.

The Christian woman can even accept aging with humor! As Ethel Barrymore said, "Wrinkles should only indicate where smiles have been."[11] Evan Esar has collected and shared these quips so we will not take ourselves or aging too seriously:

- A woman's age is like the speedometer of a used car for sale; it has been set back, but you don't know how far.

- It's always difficult to tell a woman's age – at least, it is for her.

- When a woman begins to show her age, she begins to hide it.

- Don't complain that you aren't as young as you used to be: you never were.

- Many a woman grows old before her time trying to look young after her time.

- Age creeps up on a woman, but never quite catches up with her.[12]

Beauty doesn't have to fade with age. Many fine objects of craftsmanship – jewelry, sculptures, woodworks – take on a beautiful patina with age. Only with time and pressure does a common piece of coal become a sparkling diamond. So too can aging bring out special beauty in a woman. Deirdre Budge said,

> There is only one kind of beauty that can transcend time, and many women possess it. It is, of course, beauty of the spirit that lights the eyes and transforms even a plain woman into a beautiful one. Women with wit, charm, and warmth, who are interested in others and forget themselves, and accept each stage of life gracefully, are the lasting beauties of this world – and the happiest.[13]

Which New Body?

A brand-new body – at one time or another perhaps each of us has wished for the chance! An episode of the TV show *The Twilight Zone* with Rod Serling told the story of a futuristic place where people with worn-out bodies could get new, vibrant ones. Wanting new bodies to begin again, an elderly couple comes in with their life savings. Unfortunately, all their money would pay for only one transformation. They decide that the wife will become the lucky recipient. In she goes as an old lady, and out she comes – lithe, shapely, gorgeous, youthful – and out of place next to her elderly husband.

Next, the couple decide that it would be better for the husband to have the young body, so she is returned to her original state. He enters, and later out he comes – leaping, muscular, manly – and disconnected from his elderly wife. Finally, they decide that it would be best if they remain as they were. The man is returned to his former self, and they walk out, hand in hand.

This couple's frustration symbolizes our frustration with our bodies. We try to match our aging bodies with our eternal spirits. Our souls live forever; why don't our earthly bodies? Paul urges us to look in the ageless mirror of eternity:

> Therefore we do not lose heart. Though outwardly we are wasting away, yet inwardly we are being renewed day by day.

For our light and momentary troubles are achieving for us an eternal glory that far outweighs them all. So we fix our eyes not on what is seen, but on what is unseen. For what is seen is temporary, but what is unseen is eternal. Now we know that if the earthly tent we live in is destroyed, we have a building from God, an eternal house in heaven, not built by human hands (2 Corinthians 4:16-5:1).

One day, if we are faithful to God, our bodies will be transformed to match our eternal spirits. We already have been created in His immortal image, our spirits bearing His eternal stamp. But when Jesus returns, we will have the privilege of being like Him in body as well. We will no longer be subject to dying and death, sickness and wrinkles, flab and age spots. Our bodies will be beautiful and complete. "But we know that when he appears, we shall be like him, for we shall see him as he is" (1 John 3:2). No matter what our bodies look like on Earth, they will be new and heavenly. We will be transformed into His image (2 Corinthians 3:18).

Inside Out

1. What are some examples of our society putting more importance on the present rather than the past?

2. How were old age and early death viewed in the Bible?

3. What important roles did the Bible hold for the elderly?

4. In Scripture, how was respect shown the aged?

5. How can we more easily accept our looks as we age?

6. What monetary values were people given as they aged in Leviticus 27:1-8? Note how women, although having overall less "value" than men, had proportionally more value in old age. Why do you think this was true?

7. What two men of faith did not seem to be physically affected by age (Deuteronomy 34:7; Joshua 14:11)?

8. What women have their ages mentioned in Genesis 23:1 and Luke 2:37? What important roles did they play even though they were older?

9. Name the frailties of aging mentioned in Ecclesiastes 12:1-7.

10. What was "Corban," and how did the Jews misuse it (Mark 7:9-13)?

The Way It Was

To COLOR OR COVER?

When Jesus proclaimed, "[Y]ou cannot make even one hair white or black" (Matthew 5:36), He was explaining how we cannot change our hair color by our own inherent power, much less by taking an oath. But since ancient times, women have been using whatever means they could to color or cover their hair. Take, for example, this ancient Egyptian recipe for preventing gray hair:

> One part paws of dog
> One part kernels of date
> One part hoof of donkey
> Cook ingredients thoroughly in earthenware pot and anoint head.[14]

Egyptian women also used sage, henna, indigo and chamomile to transform their hair color. In Rome it was the law for prostitutes to dye their hair yellow or wear yellow wigs. The fashion spread until many women in society were sporting golden tresses. To keep up with the demand, slaves' hair was imported from Germany to make the yellow wigs.[15]

Men and women among the ancients wore hair pieces. Sometimes they resorted to wigs when they just wanted a change of color or when their hair was destroyed by unskillful dyeing or the overuse of hot tongs.[16] Egyptian royalty wore top-heavy wigs made of black or dark brown sheep wool with decorative beads, gold and jewels, as well as a high crown. Some even boasted wigs wrought entirely from precious stones and jewels – enamels, turquoise, lapis lazuli, silver and gold.[17]

The most amazing lesson from the Bible about hair, though, is that the Lord knows us so well that He even knows the number of hairs on our head (Matthew 10:30; Luke 12:7).

Chapter 13

TOWARD THE ULTIMATE MAKEOVER

> *"Jesus says, 'I love you just the way you are. And I love you too much to let you stay the way you are.'"*
>
> Chris Lyons[1]

HAVE YOU EVER wondered what happens to those people we see on television and in the magazines who have makeovers? Months or years later, do the people who had those makeovers still look good, using the tips and techniques they have learned? Or do they revert to their "before" pictures – or worse?

Some makeovers are even advertised as the "Ultimate Makeover," giving the impression that nothing could ever improve on the finished product. The fact is that even people who have a makeover must work to maintain their new look. Benjamin Franklin said, "When you're finished changing, you're finished."[2] Most changes are not permanent. If a makeover is just a one-time event, not an ongoing process of improvement, the beauty gained in the makeover will soon be lost. Just as musical instruments must be constantly tuned to maintain their beautiful sound, so too must we work to keep ourselves in tune.

Changing and Growing

Fine-tuning our lives spiritually is even more important. Being buried in baptism does make us over as new creatures, but what happens after that? We must keep moving forward and growing. Growing isn't a fixed state but a process of working toward the ultimate. Does the ultimate mean perfection? No, perfection is beyond our reach. When Paul wrote, "Aim for perfection" (2 Corinthians 13:11), he meant we should work toward the goal of maturity and completeness. We need to echo Paul's thoughts from Philippians 3:12-14.

> Not that I have already obtained all this, or have already been made perfect, but I press on to take hold of that for which Jesus Christ took hold of me. Brothers, I do not consider myself yet to have taken hold of it. But one thing I do: Forgetting what is behind and straining toward what is ahead, I press on toward the goal to win the prize for which God has called me heavenward in Christ Jesus.

In reaching toward that goal of maturity, we must be pliable in God's hands like clay in a potter's hands. By learning God's will through Bible study, talking to Him through prayer, fellowshipping with other Christians, and totally relying on Him for our needs, we can be molded and shaped as clay by the Master Potter. We are called from what we were to what we can become through Him. Like the old saying, "I ain't all I should be, I ain't all I could be, but thank God I ain't what I wuz!"

Perhaps we want to change, but we are trying to do it on our own rather than with God's strength and guidance. Or maybe we are too busy trying to change someone else. We've heard about the woman who tried to change her husband for 15 years, then divorced him because he wasn't the man she married! We cannot change other people, and alone we certainly cannot change ourselves. We need help from the greatest Changer of mankind. We need God, and He is the One "who is able to do immeasurably more than all we ask or imagine, according to his power that is at work within us" (Ephesians 3:20). God's power within us can mold us into something better than we ever dreamed. He is never finished with us, either. We always have areas that need improvement. He is constantly making us over. We are told to "continue to work out your salvation with fear and trembling, for it is God who works in you to will and to act according to his good purpose" (Philippians 2:12-13).

Model Makeovers

Just look what God's Son did for some of the people He encountered. They wanted to change, and that's when the Lord began their transformation. The tax collector Zacchaeus started restoring four times any money he had stolen and giving half his wealth to the poor. A weeping, sinful woman learned that forgiveness was sweeter than the perfume she poured on Jesus' feet. A blind man received his sight and began to see who Jesus really was. Countless other people admitted their inadequacy and the Lord's all-encompassing power to change. Their change started with a willing and obedient heart, and there was plenty of room to grow.

Peter knew firsthand about growing. Transformed from an impulsive fisherman to a powerful preacher, he knew God's makeover power. Later Peter listed some traits of the Christian in rather a stair-step order, beginning with faith, the basis on which we begin, and arriving at love, the final goal and greatest trait. He admonished us:

> For this very reason, make every effort to add to your faith goodness; and to goodness, knowledge; and to knowledge, self-control; and to self-control, perseverance; and to perseverance, godliness; and to godliness, brotherly kindness; and to brotherly kindness, love. For if you possess these qualities in increasing measure, they will keep you from being ineffective and unproductive in your knowledge of our Lord Jesus Christ (2 Peter 1:5-8).

Peter took for granted that we cannot add all these traits at once, but that they must be added progressively. He later told us, "But grow in the grace and knowledge of our Lord and Savior Jesus Christ" (3:18).

Paul was no stranger to growth and change, either. In one of the most dramatic about-faces in the Bible, Paul changed from killing Christians to probably dying with them. (Tradition says he was beheaded.) Remembering his own guilt, he encouraged Christians to forget the past and press toward the prize of heaven (Philippians 3:12-14). In Galatians, he enumerated the fruits of the Spirit and contrasted them with the acts of the sinful nature:

> But the fruit of the Spirit is love, joy, peace, patience, kindness, goodness, faithfulness, gentleness and self-control. Against such things there is no law. Those who belong to Christ Jesus have crucified the sinful nature with its passions and desires. Since we live by the Spirit, let us keep in step with the Spirit (Galatians 5:22-25).

Sadly, we often fall out of step with the Spirit. Change is slow, and we are impatient. We are accustomed to drive-in service and instant food, and we want quick change. Counselor Larry Crabb writes:

> The process of change is something like a walk across America. Every step is progress but there's such a long way to go. The trick is to be encouraged with how far you've come without letting pride weaken your determination to continue on. An honest look at the distance yet to be covered should cure the most advanced saint of conceit."[3]

We have so far to go spiritually, yet God will guide us every step of the way, no matter how long it takes.

The Ultimate Makeover

We have described spiritual makeovers as a gradual process of growth. One day, however, there will be a split-second transformation of all people for all time. In explaining that our physical bodies cannot enter heaven, Paul wrote:

> Listen, I tell you a mystery. We will not all sleep, but we will be changed – in a flash, in the twinkling of an eye, at the last trumpet. For the trumpet will sound, the dead will be raised imperishable, and we will be changed. For the perishable must clothe itself with the imperishable, and the mortal with immortality. When the perishable has been clothed with the im-

perishable, and the mortal with immortality, then the saying that is written will come true: 'Death has been swallowed up in victory' (1 Corinthians 15:51-54).

This will be the final victory over death, aging and disease. Through John in the book of Revelation, the Lord gave a vivid description of the battle between good and evil and the final victory of Christ and His church. Interestingly, John used the physical beauty of a woman to describe the supreme moment when the body of believers will meet their Redeemer. John wrote, "Then I saw a new heaven and a new earth, for the first heaven and the first earth had passed away, and there was no longer any sea. I saw the Holy City, the new Jerusalem, coming down out of heaven from God, prepared as a bride beautifully dressed for her husband" (Revelation 21:1-2).

Have you ever seen an ugly bride? Whether women are beautiful from the excitement of the festive occasion or the promise of joy to come, it is difficult to imagine a sad or an ugly bride! This passage is even more fitting when we understand the preparation of a bride for her wedding in John's day.

On her special day, the Hebrew bride was adorned like a queen. She was bathed, anointed with perfumes, and groomed with cosmetics by her companions (Ephesians 5:26).[4] She might have worn fine linen, elaborately embroidered and perhaps decorated with gold thread woven into the garment. Her hair was braided with precious stones (Psalm 45:14-15; Isaiah 61:10). She wore a traditional headdress, heavy with jewels and gold ornaments. Gold coins became a part of the headdress, sometimes becoming a portion of the bride's dowry.[5] These jewels and ornaments were such a part of the ceremony that they could not be forgotten (Jeremiah 2:32).

As a bride is joyful, pure and prepared, so will the church be ready to enjoy a happy and peaceful communion with God in heaven, their wonderful new home:

Now the dwelling of God is with men, and he will live with them. They will be his people, and God himself will be with them and be their God. He will wipe every tear from their eyes. There will be no more death or mourning or crying or pain, for the old order of things has passed away. He who was seated on the throne said, "I am making everything new!" (Revelation 21:3-5).

At that glorious time, when the Lord changes us and makes us new, we will have the ultimate makeover!

Inside Out

1. What did Paul mean when he said, "Aim for perfection"?

2. List the Christian traits in 2 Peter 1:5-8, and explain how they build on each other.

3. List and define the fruit of the Spirit in Galatians 5:22.

4. How did Paul change from a persecutor to being persecuted (1 Timothy 1:12-17; 2 Corinthians 11:22-29)?

5. Compare these references about spiritual infancy and growth from Paul (Ephesians 4:11-16) and Peter (1 Peter 2:1-2).

6. What was said to be growing in each of these scriptures?

    Colossians 1:6, 10; 2 Thessalonians 1:3

7. What new things are involved when we become Christians?

    Romans 6:1-7; 7:6; 1 Corinthians 11:25; 2 Corinthians 3:6; 5:17; Galatians 6:15; Ephesians 4:23-24; Colossians 3:10; Hebrews 10:20

8. Besides the preparation of the Jewish bride, what other wedding customs do these scriptures show?

    Genesis 29:22-30; Judges 14:10-18; Song of Solomon 3:11; Matthew 22:1-14; 25:1-13; John 2:1-11

9. What are some ways to become more mature?

    Hebrews 6:1-2 ; James 1:2-5

10. What will happen at the ultimate makeover?

BEAUTY ATTITUDE SURVEY RESULTS

The purpose of this informal survey is not to make sweeping conclusions but rather to see what a sampling of women in the church think about these beauty issues. Responses were taken from 100 Christian women ages 20 and over from Alabama, Arkansas, Florida, Georgia, Indiana, Kansas, Maryland, Michigan, Mississippi, Nebraska, New Mexico, North Carolina, Ohio, Oregon, Tennessee, Texas, Washington and West Virginia. Much appreciation goes to all the women who anonymously participated and to the people who coordinated their efforts.

1. Do you think too much emphasis is placed on physical appearance in today's world?

Yes – 94   No – 6

2. Do you dread the inevitable wrinkles, "redistributed" weight and gray hair that come with getting older?

Not at all – 19   A little – 68   A lot – 13

3. Have you ever wished you could look like the models in magazines?

Often – 7   Sometimes – 65   Never – 28

4. Have you talked about weight, calories, diet or exercise in the last week?

Yes – 89   No – 9   NA – 2

5. How would you rate your body image, i.e. the way you see your body?

Low (frumpy) – 23   Average (OK) – 74
High (fantastic) – 3

6. How important are designer labels in clothes and accessories to you?

Small importance – 77   Average importance – 22
Great importance – 1

7. If you had to tell your age or your weight, which would you rather tell?

Age – 87   Weight – 12   NA – 1

8. If you had to generalize just one image during your growing-up years, do you think your parents or care givers gave you a positive or negative feeling about your body?

Positive – 68   Negative – 28   NA – 4

9. If you could, would you undergo cosmetic plastic surgery on any part of your body? (This does not count repairs for birth defects or disfigurement from accidents or disease.)

Yes – 26   No – 74

10. Do you think you need to lose weight right now?

Yes – 79   No – 21

My hope is that this study has caused you to reconsider your attitudes about beauty. God commands that our hearts and attitudes must change for the better to be pleasing to Him. He can transform our attitudes toward our appearance. God can help us to develop a healthier body image, no matter what our past. We can grow to the point where we no longer have to compete with the model on the magazine cover or the neighbor down the street. Moderation can dictate the style of our clothes as well as the time and money we spend on beauty. We can learn to be more active without being driven. Food doesn't have to control us, but rather we can control our focus on it. And we don't have to dread growing older, but we can look at aging as growing up.

These changes won't come overnight but neither do *real* makeovers. God's makeover plan calls for a continual renewal of our minds and a maturing of our attitudes. Only with His help can we grow from the inside out. Although it is important to look good, it is more important to look to God. Only He can make us beautiful where it counts.

End Notes

Chapter One

1. Debra Evans, *Beauty and the Best* (Colorado Springs: Focus on the Family Publishing, 1993), pp. 164-165.

2. J.P.V.D. Balsdon, *Roman Women: Their History and Habits* (New York: Barnes & Noble, 1962), p. 258.

3. J.D. Douglas and Merrill C. Tenney, eds., *The New International Dictionary of the Bible* (Grand Rapids: Zondervan, 1987), p. 122.

4. Madeleine S. Miller and J. Lane Miller, *Harper's Bible Dictionary* (New York: Harper & Row, 1973), p. 242.

Chapter Two

1. Ralph Woods, ed., *The World Treasury of Religious Quotations* (New York: Hawthorn Books, 1966), p. 47.

2. Judith Couchman, *The Woman Behind the Mirror* (Nashville: Broadman & Holman Publishers, 1997), pp. 48-51.

3. Walter Duckat, *Beggar to King: All the Occupations of Biblical Times* (Garden City, N.Y.: Doubleday, 1968), p. 151.

4. Madeleine S. Miller and J. Lane Miller, *Harper's Bible Dictionary* (New York: Harper & Row, 1973), p. 449.

5. Duckat, op. cit., p. 151.

6. Edith Deen, *The Bible's Legacy for Womanhood* (Garden City, N.Y.: Doubleday, 1969), p. 63.

7. J.D. Douglas and Merrill C. Tenney, eds., *The New International Dictionary of the Bible* (Grand Rapids: Zondervan, 1987), p. 663.

Chapter Three

1. Ralph Woods, ed., *The World Treasury of Religious Quotations* (New York: Hawthorn Books, 1966), p. 47.

2. William Hendriksen, *New Testament Commentary: Exposition of the Pastoral Epistles* (Grand Rapids: Baker Book House, 1970), pp. 106-107.

3. William Barclay, *The Letters to the Corinthians* (Philadelphia: Westminster Press, 1956), p. 62.

4. Mary Ann Mayo, *Looking Good But Feeling Bad* (Ann Arbor: Servant Publications, 1992), pp. 201-202.

5. Ibid., pp. 202-203.

6. Judith Couchman, *The Woman Behind the Mirror* (Nashville: Broadman & Holman Publishers, 1997), pp. 120-121.

7. Madeleine S. Miller and J. Lane Miller, *Harper's Bible Dictionary* (New York: Harper & Row, 1973), p. 501.

8. Walter Duckat, *Beggar to King: All the Occupations of Biblical Times* (Garden City, N.Y.: Doubleday, 1968), p. 169.

9. Miller and Miller, op. cit., p. 502.

10. J.D. Douglas and Merrill C. Tenney, eds., *The New International Dictionary of the Bible* (Grand Rapids: Zondervan, 1987), p. 728.

Chapter Four

1. Victoria Jackson and Paddy Calistro, *Redefining Beauty* (New York: Warner Books, 1993), p. 16.

2. Susan Faludi, *Backlash* (New York: Crown Publishers, 1991), p. 202.

3. "Your Mind & Body Viewer's Guide," *Health* (July/Aug. 1996), p. 61.

4. Sara Halprin, *Look at My Ugly Face* (New York: Viking, 1995), p. 59.

5. Faludi, op. cit., p. 203.

6. Naomi Wolf, *The Beauty Myth* (London: Chatto & Windus, 1990), p. 223.

7. Diagram adapted from Rita Freedman, *Bodylove: Learning to Like Our Looks and Ourselves* (New York: Harper & Row, 1988), p. 21.

8. Ibid., pp. 21-22.

9. Susan Jacoby, "The Body Image Blues," *Family Circle* (Feb. 1, 1990), p. 41.

10. Freedman, op. cit., pp. 50-51.

11. Wolf, op. cit., p. 191.

12. Mary Pipher, *Reviving Ophelia: Saving the Selves of Adolescent Girls* (New York: Ballantine Books, 1994), p. 279.

13. Teri Twitty-Villani, *Appearances Speak Louder Than Words* (Portland, Ore.: Voyager Press, 1992), p. 80.

14. Freedman, op. cit., p. 72.

15. Kim Boyce and Ken Abraham, *Beauty to Last a Lifetime: A Step by Step Guide to Inner and Outer Beauty for Teenage Girls* (Elgin, Ill.: Chariot Family Publishing, 1992), p. 69.

16. Walter Duckat, *Beggar to King: All the Occupations of Biblical Times* (Garden City, N.Y.: Doubleday, 1968), p. 124.

17. Madeleine S. Miller and J. Lane Miller, *Harper's Bible Dictionary* (New York: Harper & Row, 1973), p. 208.

18. J.D. Douglas and Merrill C. Tenney, eds., *The New International Dictionary of the Bible* (Grand Rapids: Zondervan, 1987), pp. 362, 720.

Chapter Five

1. Judith Couchman, *The Woman Behind the Mirror* (Nashville: Broadman & Holman, 1997), p. 83.

2. Gleason L. Archer, *Encyclopedia of Bible Difficulties* (Grand Rapids: Zondervan, 1982), p. 80.

3. Archer, op. cit., p. 262.

4. Guy N. Woods, *A Commentary on the New Testament Epistles of Peter, John and Jude* (Nashville: Gospel Advocate Co., 1973), pp. 88-89.

5. *Jesus and His Times* (Pleasantville, N.Y.: Reader's Digest Association, 1987), p. 80.

6. J.D. Douglas and Merrill C. Tenney, eds., *The New International Dictionary of the Bible* (Grand Rapids: Zondervan, 1987), p. 128.

7. Madeleine S. Miller and J. Lane Miller, *Harper's Bible Dictionary* (New York: Harper & Row, 1973), p. 63.

8. Ralph Gower, *The New Manners and Customs of Bible Times* (Chicago: Moody Press, 1987), p. 48.

9. Douglas and Tenney, op. cit., p. 128.

10. Miller and Miller, loc. cit., p. 63.

Chapter Six

1. Judith Couchman, *The Woman Behind the Mirror* (Nashville: Broadman & Holman, 1997), p. 72.

2. William Sanford LaSor, *Daily Life in Bible Times* (Cincinnati: Standard, 1966), p. 32.

3. Arthur Marwick, *Beauty in History* (London: Thames and Hudson, 1988), pp. 65, 67.

4. Ibid., pp. 68-69.

5. Ibid., pp. 60-61.

6. Ibid., p. 71.

7. Ibid., p. 77.

8. Ibid., p. 81.

9. Ibid., p. 81.

10. Ibid., pp. 185-186.

11. Ibid., p. 199.

12. Ibid., pp. 295, 390-391, 397.

13. Rita Freedman, *Bodylove: Learning to Like Our Looks and Ourselves* (New York: Harper & Row, 1988), p. 114.

14. Ralph Gower, *The New Manners and Customs of Bible Times* (Chicago: Moody Press, 1987), p. 15.

15. J.D. Douglas and Merrill C. Tenney, eds., *The New International Dictionary of the Bible* (Grand Rapids: Zondervan, 1987), p. 285.

16. Gower, op. cit., p. 250.

17. Douglas and Tenney, loc. cit., p. 285.

18. Madeleine S. Miller and J. Lane Miller, *Harper's Bible Dictionary* (New York: Harper & Row, 1973), p. 679.

Chapter Seven

1. Judith Couchman, *The Woman Behind the Mirror* (Nashville: Broadman & Holman, 1997), p. 64.

2. H.C. Leupold, *Exposition of Genesis, Vol. 2* (Grand Rapids: Baker Book House, 1942), p. 793.

3. John T. Willis, *Genesis* (Abilene: ACU Press, 1984), p. 337.

4. Judith Rodin, *Body Traps* (New York: William Morrow and Company, 1992), p. 95.

5. Naomi Wolf, *The Beauty Myth* (London: Chatto & Windus, 1990), p. 57.

6. Rodin, op. cit., pp. 102-103.

7. Debra Evans, *Beauty and the Best* (Colorado Springs: Focus on the Family Publishing, 1993), pp. 18-19.

8. Rodin, op. cit., pp. 100-120.

9. *Food for Thought* (Edina, Minn.: Heartland Samplers, 1994), p. 66.

10. Annie Chapman and Maureen Rank, *Smart Women Keep It Simple* (Minneapolis: Bethany House, 1992), pp. 127-128.

11. Rodin, op. cit., p. 112.

12. J.P.V.D. Balsdon, *Roman Women: Their History and Habits* (New York: Barnes & Noble, 1962), p. 263.

13. J.D. Douglas and Merrill C. Tenney, eds., *The New International Dictionary of the Bible* (Grand Rapids: Zondervan, 1987), p. 525.

14. Balsdon, op. cit., p. 263.

Chapter Eight

1. Charla Krupp, "What Price Beauty?" *Glamour* (April 1991), pp. 296-297.

2. Debra Evans, *Beauty and the Best* (Colorado Springs: Focus on the Family Publishing, 1993), pp. 44-51.

3. Naomi Wolf, *The Beauty Myth* (London: Chatto & Windus, 1990), p. 181.

4. Ibid., p. 203.

5. Judith Couchman, *The Woman Behind the Mirror* (Nashville: Broadman and Holman, 1997), pp. 70-71.

6. Glenn D. Kiltler, *Let's Travel in the Congo* (Chicago, Children's Press, 1965), p. 46.

7. John Woodforde, *The History of Vanity* (New York: St. Martin's Press, 1992), p. 51.

8. Ibid., p. 19.

9. Couchman, op. cit., p. 71.

10. Arthur Marwick, *Beauty in History* (London: Thames and Hudson, 1988), p. 299.

11. Nancy Roberts, *Breaking All the Rules* (Middlesex, England: Viking Penguin, 1985), p. 197.

12. Woodforde, op. cit., p. 118.

13. Rudolph Bell, *Holy Anorexia* (Chicago: The University of Chicago Press, 1987), p. 23.

14. Jenny Tesar, "The Growing Popularity of Cosmetic Surgery," *American Annual 1998* (Danbury, Conn.: Grolier Year Book, 1998),

pp. 67-68.

15. "The Price of Vanity," *U.S. News & World Report* (Oct. 14, 1996), pp. 72-80.

16. Madeleine S. Miller and J. Lane Miller, *Harper's Bible Dictionary* (New York: Harper & Row, 1973), p. 115.

17. Walter Duckat, *Beggar to King: All the Occupations of Biblical Times* (Garden City, N.Y.: Doubleday, 1968), p. 7.

18. Edith Deen, *The Bible's Legacy for Womanhood* (Garden City, N.Y.: Doubleday, 1969), pp. 128-129.

19. Duckat, loc. cit., p. 7.

20. Pearl Binder, *Muffs and Morals* (New York: William Morrow, 1954), p. 86.

21. J.P.V.D. Balsdon, *Roman Women: Their History and Habits* (New York: Barnes & Noble, 1962), p. 262.

Chapter Nine

1. Evan Esar, *20,000 Quips and Quotes* (Garden City, N.Y.: Doubleday, 1968), p. 145.

2. Carol Brockway, *2001 Quick Ways to Look and Feel Your Best* (Eugene, Ore.: Harvest House, 1993), p. 75.

3. *Reader's Digest Great Encyclopedia Dictionary* (Pleasantville, N.Y.: Reader's Digest Associates, 1966), p. 2027.

4. William Coleman, *Today's Handbook of Bible Times & Customs* (Minneapolis: Bethany House, 1984), p. 51.

5. Doris Pooser, *Always in Style* (Los Altos, Calif.: Crisp Publications, 1989), p. 157.

6. Barbara Weiland and Leslie Wood, *Clothes Sense* (Portland, Ore.: Palmer/Pletsch Associates, 1991), p. 70.

7. Pamela Redmond Satron, *Dressing Smart: The Woman's Guide to Style* (New York: Doubleday, 1990), pp. 122-123.

8. "What a Deal!" *Family Circle* (April 4, 1995), pp. 72-77.

9. Nancy Eichman, "Consumer Madness," *Christian Woman* (Nov./Dec. 1994), p. 42.

10. Edith Deen, *The Bible's Legacy for Womanhood* (Garden City, N.Y.: Doubleday, 1969), p. 125.

11. J.P.V.D. Balsdon, *Roman Women: Their History and Habits* (New York: Barnes & Noble, 1962), p. 254.

12. Deen, op. cit., p. 126.

Chapter Ten

1. Elaine St. James, *Simplify Your Life* (New York: Hyperion, 1994), p. 161.

2. Stormie Omartian, *Better Body Management* (Nashville: Sparrow Press, 1993), p. 20.

3. Peter Francis and Lorna Francis, *Real Exercise for Real People* (Rocklin, Calif.: Prima Publishing, 1996), p. 2.

4. Herbert Lockyer, *All the Men of the Bible / All the Women of the Bible* (Grand Rapids: Zondervan, 1996), p. 19.

5. Walter Duckat, *Beggar to King: All the Occupations of Biblical Times* (Garden City, N. Y.: Doubleday, 1968), p. 309.

6. *Prevention's All New! No Diet, No Willpower Weight-Loss System* (Emmaus, Pa.: Rodale Press, 1995), p. 43.

7. James "Doc" Blakely, *Doc Blakely's Push Button Wit* (Houston: Rich Publishing Co., 1988), p. 109.

8. Omartian, op. cit., p. 63.

9. Rita Freedman, *Bodylove: Learning to Like Our Looks and Ourselves* (New York: Harper & Row, 1988), p. 122.

10. Francis and Francis, op. cit., p. 23.

11. Katie Newby, "Rebuilding God's Temple," *Christian Woman* (July/Aug. 1993), p. 56.

12. Neva Coyle, *Overcoming the Dieting Dilemma* (Minneapolis, Bethany House, 1991), p. 148.

13. Freedman, op. cit., pp. 123-125.

14. Walter Duckat, *Beggar to King: All the Occupations of Biblical Times* (Garden City, N. Y.: Doubleday, 1968), p. 40.

15. Ralph Gower, *The New Manners and Customs of Bible Times* (Chicago: Moody Press, 1987), pp. 108-109.

16. J.D. Douglas and Merrill C. Tenney, eds., *The New International Dictionary of the Bible* (Grand Rapids: Zondervan, 1987), p. 718.

Chapter Eleven

1. Evan Esar, *20,000 Quips and Quotes* (Garden City, N. Y.: Doubleday, 1968), p. 253.

2. Keith Main, *Prayer and Fasting* (New York: Carlton Press, 1971), pp. 21-22.

3. Main, op. cit., pp. 58-59.

4. Richard J. Foster, *Celebration of Discipline: The Path to Spiritual Growth* (San Francisco: Harper & Row, 1978), p. 44.

5. Doyle Kee, "Fasting Revisited," *Gospel Advocate* (Aug. 1991), pp. 37-38.

6. Rudolph Bell, *Holy Anorexia* (Chicago: University of Chicago Press, 1987), pp. 20, 174-175.

7. Stormie Omartian, *Better Body Management* (Nashville: Sparrow Press, 1993), pp. 116-118.

8. Gwen Shamblin, *The Weigh Down Diet* (New York: Doubleday, 1997), p. 100.

9. JoAnna M. Lund, *Healthy Exchanges Cookbook* (New York: G.P. Putnam's Sons, 1995), pp. 50-51.

10. Rich McLawhorn, "Exchanged Values," *Daily Wisdom 8-27-97* (SISTERS e-mail list).

11. Edith Deen, *The Bible's Legacy for Womanhood* (Garden City, N.Y.: Doubleday, 1969), pp. 191-192.

Chapter Twelve

1. *The Reader's Digest Great Encyclopedic Dictionary* (Pleasantville, N.Y.: Reader's Digest Association, 1966), p. 2023.

2. Michael Maron, *Makeover Miracles* (New York: Crown Publishers, 1994), p. 79.

3. William Cole, ed. *When You Consider the Alternative: Enlightening and Amusing Words on Age and Aging* (New York: St. Martin's Griffin, 1996), p. 25.

4. Stephen Sapp, *Full of Years* (Nashville: Abingdon Press, 1987), pp. 39-40, 44-45.

5. Ibid., p. 67.

6. Ibid., pp. 69-71.

7. Ibid., pp. 72-75.

8. Ibid., p. 76.

9. Ibid., pp. 148-149.

10. Rita Freedman. *Bodylove: Learning to Like Our Looks and Ourselves* (New York: Harper & Row, 1988), p. 186.

11. *The Reader's Digest Great Encyclopedic Dictionary*, p. 2033.

12. Evan Esar, *20,000 Quips and Quotes* (Garden City, N.Y.: Doubleday, 1968), pp. 19-21, 38.

13. Kim Boyce and Ken Abraham, *Beauty to Last a Lifetime: A*

Step by Step Guide to Inner and Outer Beauty for Teenage Girls (Elgin, Ill.: Chariot Family Publishing, 1992), p. 185.

14. Pearl Binder, *Muffs and Morals* (New York: William Morrow, 1954), p. 99.

15. Ibid., p. 101.

16. J.P.V.D. Balsdon, *Roman Women: Their History and Habits* (New York: Barnes & Noble, 1962), p. 258.

17. Binder, op. cit., pp. 99-101, 133.

Chapter Thirteen

1. Kim Boyce and Ken Abraham, *Beauty to Last a Lifetime: A Step by Step Guide to Inner and Outer Beauty for Teenage Girls* (Elgin, Ill.: Chariot Family Publishing, 1992), p. 17.

2. Harvey Diamond and Marilyn Diamond, *Fit for Life II: Living Health* (New York: Warner Books, 1989), p. xvii.

3. Larry Crabb, *Inside Out* (Colorado Springs: NavPress, 1989), p. 179.

4. Ralph Gower, *The New Manners and Customs of Bible Times* (Chicago: Moody Press, 1987), p. 66.

5. J.D. Douglas and Merrill C. Tenney, eds., *The New International Dictionary of the Bible* (Grand Rapids: Zondervan, 1987), p. 1059.